KJV Word Puzzles

King James Bible
Vocabulary Practice

Reviews are very important to a small business like ours. Please take a moment to leave us some feedback, wherever you purchased this book. Thank you!

About This Book

- Definitions for the words in this book are not intended to be precise or all-inclusive. The definitions are simplified as the goal is to give the reader *more understanding while reading* rather than glossing over unfamiliar words.

- Word meanings have changed over time, so some words that are still commonly used in today's English had different definitions in 1611. Some spelling for words may have also changed, and other words use the British spelling rather than the American spelling. The definitions and spellings in this book follow the originals used in the Bible, and therefore may be archaic or British.

- Some words have multiple meanings depending on the context and/or may be used as multiple grammatical parts of speech. Because of this, the user may find multiple instances of the same word, or more than one variant from the same root.
An example is the word "counsel":

COUNSEL, noun [Latin , to consult; to ask, to assail.]
1. Advice; opinion, or instruction, given upon request or otherwise, for directing the judgment or conduct of another; opinion given upon deliberation or consultation.
Every purpose is established by counsel Proverbs 20:5.
Thou hast not hearkened to my counsel 2 Chronicles 25:16.
2. Consultation; interchange of opinions.
We took sweet counsel together. Psalms 55:14.
3. Deliberation; examination of consequences.
They all confess that, in the working of that first cause, counsel is used, reason followed, and a way observed.
4. Prudence; deliberate opinion or judgment, or the faculty or habit of judging with caution.
The law shall perish from the priest, and counsel from the ancients. Ezekiel 7:26.
5. In a bad sense, evil advice or designs; art; machination.
The counsel of the froward is carried headlong. Job 5:13.
6. Secresy; the secrets entrusted in consultation; secret opinions or purposes. Let a man keep his own counsel
7. In a scriptural sense, purpose; design; will; decree.
What thy counsel determined before to be done. Acts 4:28.
To show the immutability of his counsel Hebrews 6:17.
8. Directions of God's word.
Thou shalt guide me by thy counsel Psalms 73:24.
9. The will of God or his truth and doctrines concerning the way of salvation.
I have not shunned to declare to you all the counsel of God. Acts 20:27.
10. Those who give counsel in law; any counselor or advocate, or any number of counselors, barristers or sergeants; as the plaintiff's counsel or the defendant's counsel
COUNSEL, verb transitive [Latin]
1. To give advice or deliberate opinion to another for the government of his conduct; to advise.
I counsel thee to buy of me gold tried in the fire. Revelations 3.
2. To exhort, warn, admonish, or instruct. We ought frequently to counsel our children against the vices of the age.
They that will not be counseled, cannot be helped.
3. To advise or recommend; as, to counsel a crime. [Not much used.]

- Definitions are primarily taken or adapted from the <u>Webster's 1828 American Dictionary of the English Language</u>. The <u>Way of Life Believer's Bible Dictionary</u> was used as a secondary source.

Old Verb Endings

ST and EST endings are used for second person, singular - thou.

Example: Genesis 2:17
But of the tree of the knowledge of good and evil, thou shalt not eat of it: for in the day that thou eat**est** thereof thou shalt surely die.

Drop the ST or EST for the modern equivalent. "Eatest" becomes "eat."

TH and ETH endings are used for the third person, singular - he, she, or it.

Example: 1 John 4:7
Beloved, let us love one another: for love is of God; and every one that lov**eth** is born of God, and know**eth** God.

Change the TH to S for the modern equivalent. "Loveth" becomes "loves" and "knoweth" becomes "knows."

PRACTICE - Convert the KJV verb to its modern equivalent. In some cases it may be necessary to change or omit other letters to spell the word correctly. Example: forgetteth = forgets.   Solution p. 125

1. ANOINTEDST _____

2. BLESSEST _____

3. BLESSETH _____

4. BORROWETH _____

5. CARETH _____

6. COMMITTEST _____

7. CREEPETH _____

8. CRIEST _____

9. DIVIDETH _____

10. EXALTEST _____

11. FILLEST _____

12. FORGAVEST _____

13. GLORIETH _____

14. LAIDST _____

15. MOVEDST _____

16. MULTIPLIEST _____

17. OPENEST _____

18. PREPAREST _____

19. READEST _____

20. RUNNETH _____

21. SMOOTHETH _____

22. SUPPLIETH _____

23. UPBRAIDETH _____

24. WINNETH _____

2

Snowflakes #1

Solution p. 123

Select a word from the word bank for each numbered clue and write it straight across the snowflake. The center letter will be the same for all 3 words on each snowflake. When you have filled in all the answers, some of the letters on the edges will spell a word from the Bible. Write each letter on its corresponding number to reveal the word.

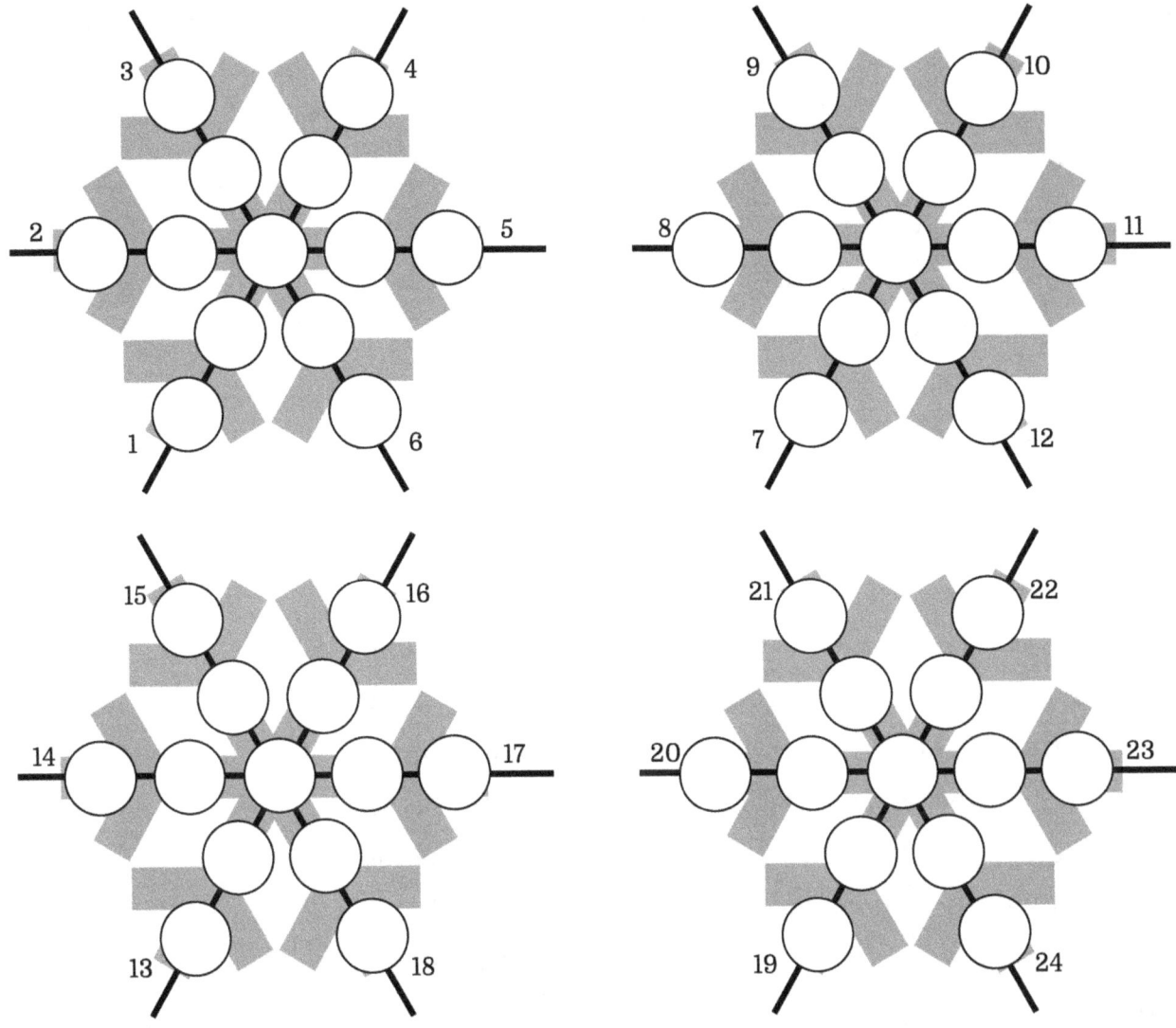

1. A wash basin
2. To eat with great eagerness
3. To separate
7. Broom
8. An outflowing
9. Speed, hurry

13. Killed
14. Worthless matter
15. To raise high
19. Two
20. To reduce low, to humble
21. A structure made of parts joined together

Word Bank

ABASE	CHAFF	FRAME	ISSUE	SEVER	SLAIN
BESOM	EXALT	HASTE	LAVER	RAVIN	TWAIN

7-Letter word from Romans 11:5 _ _ _ _ _ _ _
4 15 10 5 20 16 19

3

Anagrams #1

Each word set is an anagram of a single Bible word. Use the definition to unscramble them. Stumped? Use the reference verse for help. Solution p. 125

Example: Owing something to someone   bend diet   __indebted__

1. Upper part of a pillar (1 Kings 7:19)   preach it   _ _ _ _ _ _ _ _ _ _ _ _
2. Betraying trust (Jeremiah 3:11)   our teachers   _ _ _ _ _ _ _ _ _ _ _ _
3. The 50ᵗʰ day after Passover (Acts 20:16)   tent scope   _ _ _ _ _ _ _ _ _ _ _ _
4. Height of the body (1 Samuel 16:7)   rust tea   _ _ _ _ _ _ _ _ _ _ _ _
5. Body, matter (Psalm 139:15)   cuts beans   _ _ _ _ _ _ _ _ _ _ _ _
6. Household deities (Judges 17:5)   harp time   _ _ _ _ _ _ _ _ _ _ _ _
7. Dry food for animals (Genesis 24:32)   never drop   _ _ _ _ _ _ _ _ _ _ _ _
8. Unable to be counted (Hebrews 11:12)   alien number   _ _ _ _ _ _ _ _ _ _ _ _
9. Compulsion (1 Peter 5:2)   tint on cars   _ _ _ _ _ _ _ _ _ _ _ _
10. Covetousness (Romans 7:8)   conscience cup   _ _ _ _ _ _ _ _ _ _ _ _
11. Having patience with (Colossians 3:13)   brief groan   _ _ _ _ _ _ _ _ _ _ _ _
12. Horse drawn vehicle (Exodus 14:23)   at choir   _ _ _ _ _ _ _ _ _ _ _ _
13. That which must be (1 Corinthians 9:16)   city sense   _ _ _ _ _ _ _ _ _ _ _ _
14. Tax collector (Luke 19:2)   pain club   _ _ _ _ _ _ _ _ _ _ _ _
15. In great quantity (1 Chronicles 22:15)   tuna band   _ _ _ _ _ _ _ _ _ _ _ _
16. Afflicted (Micah 6:13)   so elated   _ _ _ _ _ _ _ _ _ _ _ _
17. Encouragement to good (1 Corinthians 14:3)   no other taxi   _ _ _ _ _ _ _ _ _ _ _ _
18. Sailors (Ezekiel 27:29)   near rims   _ _ _ _ _ _ _ _ _ _ _ _
19. Stumps left after reaping grain (Exodus 5:12)   bulb set   _ _ _ _ _ _ _ _ _ _ _ _
20. Procured to do a bad action (Acts 6:11)   rude snob   _ _ _ _ _ _ _ _ _ _ _ _
21. Maker of a last will (Hebrews 9:17)   star tote   _ _ _ _ _ _ _ _ _ _ _ _
22. Father and ruler of a family (Hebrews 7:4)   chair part   _ _ _ _ _ _ _ _ _ _ _ _
23. Compounder of medicine (Exodus 37:29)   teach or pay   _ _ _ _ _ _ _ _ _ _ _ _

Secret Word #1

Solution p. 124

Place a word from the box below on each line. The circled letters in each puzzle will spell out a secret word also found in the box (and in the Bible).

Abstain from food

Gray or white

Ponder

Low in place

Secret Word: _____

Plunder

Mild tempered, gentle

To drag

Chest area

Secret Word: _____

To put on

To beat

Dregs

Manner

Secret Word: _____

Mute

Account

To destroy

To remain

Secret Word: _____

Winged animal

Attention

Lame

Bitterness

Secret Word: _____

The rear part

To free from

Split

Believe

Secret Word: _____

BASE	FAME	HALT	MUSE	RENT
BEST	FAST	HEED	PAPS	STAY
BRAY	FOWL	HIND	PREY	TALE
DIRT	GALL	HOAR	QUIT	TROW
DREW	GIRD	LEES	RASE	WELL
DUMB	HALE	MEEK	REAP	WISE

5

Crossword 1

Solution p. 127

Across

1. Advanced (as in age)
2. Widespread disease
4. Base, despicable
5. To testify falsely, to commit perjury
7. Invited
8. Strive
12. Observant
17. To praise
19. A wide expanse
21. To do something that is expected
22. Living alone, remote
24. At a distance within view

Down

3. To cause to flee
6. A band worn on the forehead
9. Entangle
10. Scattered
11. Someone working for wages
13. Grind the teeth
14. Placed
15. As much as
16. Public civil officer
18. Change form
20. To assume a false appearance, hypocrisy
23. To make dirty

WORD BANK			
ATTENTIVE	DISSEMBLE	GNASH	SNARE
BIDDEN	EXTOL	HIRELING	SOLITARY
CONTEND	FIRMAMENT	INASMUCH	STRICKEN
DEFILE	FORSWEAR	MAGISTRATE	TRANSFIGURE
DISCOMFIT	FRONTLETS	PESTILENCE	VILE
DISPERSED	FULFILL	SITUATE	YONDER

Finish the Word #1

The following verbs have the same beginning. Can you finish them, using the definitions and word lists? The number of blanks indicates the number of missing letters.

To supply	EN _ _ _		ENCAMP
To follow	EN _ _ _		ENDUE
To bear	EN _ _ _ _		ENDURE
To pitch tents	EN _ _ _ _		ENJOIN
To lead astray	EN _ _ _ _		ENLARGE
To order or direct	EN _ _ _ _		ENSUE
To surround	EN _ _ _ _ _		ENTICE
To treat	EN _ _ _ _ _		ENTREAT
To make greater in size	EN _ _ _ _ _		ENVIRON

To urge with force	CO _ _ _ _		COMMEND
To consult	CO _ _ _ _		COMMUNE
To carry or transport	CO _ _ _ _		COMPEL
To converse	CO _ _ _ _ _		CONCEIVE
To lead the way	CO _ _ _ _ _		CONCLUDE
To firm up, as a liquid	CO _ _ _ _ _		CONDUCT
To destroy	CO _ _ _ _ _		CONFER
To strive	CO _ _ _ _ _		CONFOUND
To entrust	CO _ _ _ _ _		CONGEAL
To spoil	CO _ _ _ _ _		CONSUME
To determine	CO _ _ _ _ _ _		CONTEND
To become pregnant	CO _ _ _ _ _ _		CONVEY
To throw into disorder	CO _ _ _ _ _ _		CONVINCE
To prove guilty	CO _ _ _ _ _ _		CORRUPT

Solution p. 120

Pinwheels #1

Solution p. 119

The answer to each numbered clue will either begin or end with the letter in the center of each pinwheel. Write a word from inside to outside or outside to inside as needed.

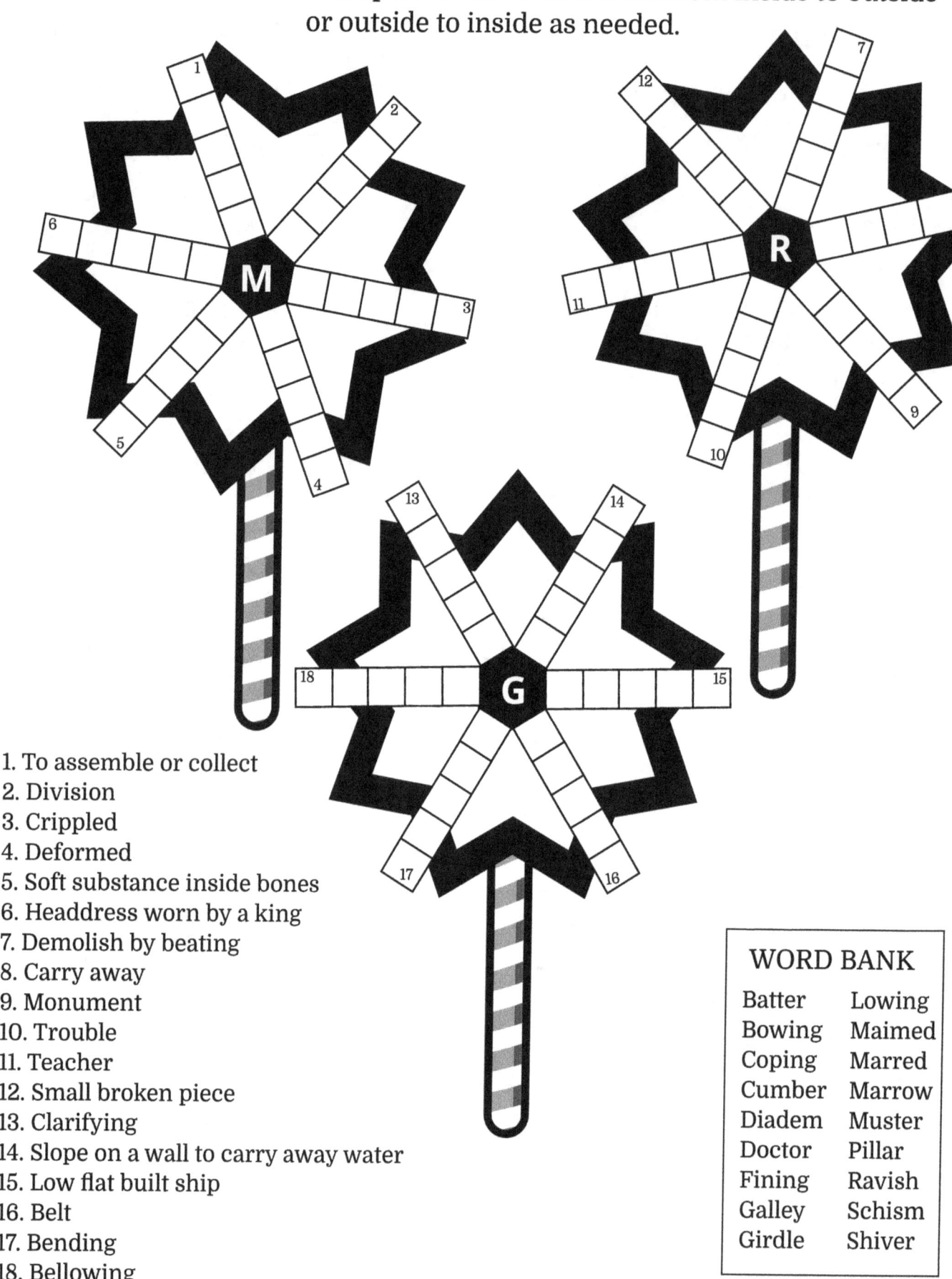

1. To assemble or collect
2. Division
3. Crippled
4. Deformed
5. Soft substance inside bones
6. Headdress worn by a king
7. Demolish by beating
8. Carry away
9. Monument
10. Trouble
11. Teacher
12. Small broken piece
13. Clarifying
14. Slope on a wall to carry away water
15. Low flat built ship
16. Belt
17. Bending
18. Bellowing

WORD BANK

Batter	Lowing
Bowing	Maimed
Coping	Marred
Cumber	Marrow
Diadem	Muster
Doctor	Pillar
Fining	Ravish
Galley	Schism
Girdle	Shiver

8

Select-A-Syllable #1

Each of the answers to the following clues is made up of two syllables that can be found in the box. Put them together and write your completed words in the spaces provided. The numbers in parentheses indicate the total number of letters in each answer. Each syllable will be used only once. Solution p. 121

1. To despise or neglect (5) _____

2. Fathered (5) _____

3. To bind by oath (6) _____

4. To make a sign to another (6) _____

5. To strike with the hand (6) _____

6. A legal judgment or announcement (6) _____

7. A chest for money (6) _____

8. To bestow (6) _____

9. Register of fact (6) _____

10. Feed trough (6) _____

11. To like (6) _____

12. Disturbance or commotion (6) _____

13. To purchase back (6) _____

14. Acting power or strength (6) _____

15. Deformity (7) _____

16. An ox (7) _____

17. Particular (7) _____

18. Taken prisoner (7) _____

19. Sad or melancholy (7) _____

20. A non-Jew (7) _____

Syllable Box

AB	CER	FUL	MAN	TAIN
AD	COF	GAT	OCK	TILE
BE	CREE	GEN	ON	TIVE
BECK	DE	GER	ORD	TUE
BLEM	DEEM	HOR	PART	TUM
BUF	DOLE	IM	RE	ULT
BULL	FER	ISH	REC	VIR
CAP	FET	JURE	SA	VOUR

Cookie Sheet #1

Use the definitions to unscramble the letters in each cookie. Write your answers on the dotted lines.

Solution p. 124

Butler

Urgent

Labor

Placed

Punish

Amazed

Sharer

Shameless

Observant

Unchangeable

Pardon

Exhaustion

Worked

Make holy

To corrupt

Follower

Crossword 2

Solution p. 127

Across
2. A part separated from the rest
4. Loose, lewd
5. Bond of connection
6. Labor
9. Surround
11. Scattered as seed
14. Pardon
16. Formal request
17. Scarcity
18. Something worn by the high priest
20. To choose
23. Settings for gemstones

Down
1. The main body of a tree
3. Chains for the feet
7. Given to excessive eating
8. To destroy
10. New convert to a religion
12. Wishing for
13. Food of any kind
15. The rear part
19. Shelter
21. Plant used to make linen
22. Care
24. One who betrays trust

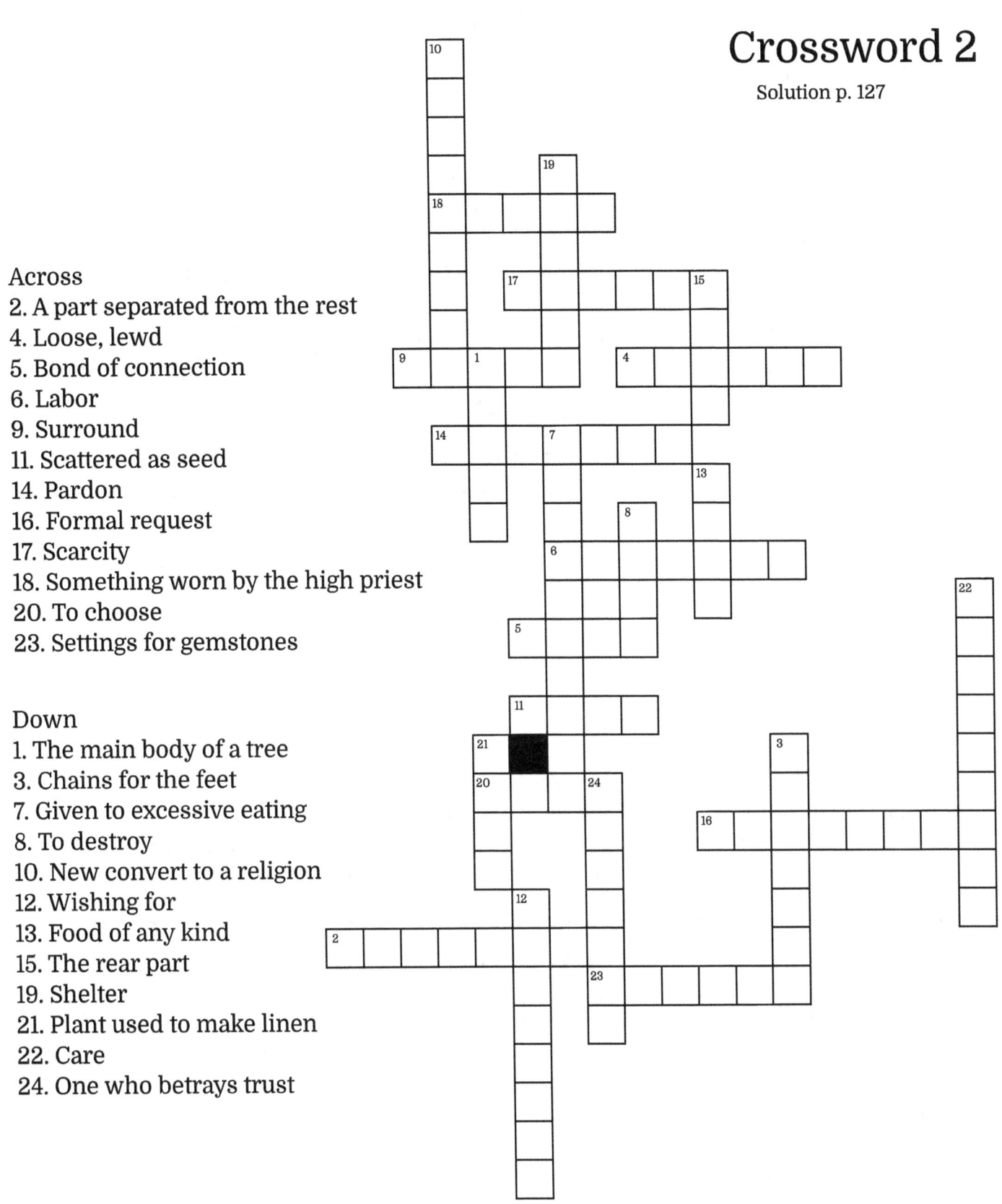

WORD BANK			
BESET	FETTERS	LIST	SOWN
COVERT	FLAX	MEAT	STOCK
DEARTH	FORGIVE	OUCHES	TRAITOR
DESIROUS	FRAGMENT	PETITION	TRAVAIL
DILIGENCE	GLUTTONOUS	PROSELYTE	WANTON
EPHOD	HIND	RASE	YOKE

11

About Bible Pronouns

The pronouns in the KJV are used to distinguish how many people are referenced.

Nominative Case

THOU is the **subject** form of the second person, personal pronoun, **singular**.

Example: Genesis 2:17
But of the tree of the knowledge of good and evil, **thou** shalt not eat of it: for in the day that thou eatest thereof **thou** shalt surely die. Here God is speaking to **Adam only**.

YE is the **subject** form of the second person, personal pronoun, **plural**.

Example: Genesis 42:9
And Joseph remembered the dreams which he dreamed of them, and said unto them, **Ye** are spies; to see the nakedness of the land **ye** are come. Joseph is speaking to **all of his brothers.**

Objective Case

THEE is the **object** form of the second person, personal pronoun, **singular**.

Example: Genesis 17:8
And I will give unto **thee**, and to thy seed after **thee**, the land wherein thou art a stranger, all the land of Canaan, for an everlasting possession; and I will be their God. God is speaking to **Abraham only**.

YOU is the **object** form of the second person, personal pronoun, **plural**.

Example: Exodus 10:16
Then Pharaoh called for Moses and Aaron in haste; and he said, I have sinned against the Lord your God, and against **you**. Pharoah is speaking to **both Moses and Aaron.**

Possessive Case

THINE means belonging to thee or relating to thee, used before a vowel sound. **(Singular)**

Example: Ezekiel 3:10
Moreover he said unto me, Son of man, all my words that I shall speak unto thee receive in **thine** heart, and hear with **thine** ears.

THY means belonging to thee or relating to thee. (Singular)

Example: Genesis 12:1
Now the Lord had said unto Abram, Get thee out of **thy** country, and from **thy** kindred, and from **thy** father's house, unto a land that I will shew thee.

YOUR means belonging to you or relating to you. **(Plural)**

Example: Joshua 24:19
And Joshua said unto the people, Ye cannot serve the Lord: for he is an holy God; he is a jealous God; he will not forgive **your** transgressions nor **your** sins.

Plural or Singular?

Based upon the pronouns used in each verse, how many people are being addressed? Write S for one person or P for more than one person.

(Solution p. 132)

_____ 1. 1 Thessalonians 1:8 For from you sounded out the word of the Lord not only in Macedonia and Achaia, but also in every place your faith to God-ward is spread abroad; so that we need not to speak any thing.

_____ 2. Acts 1:5 For John truly baptized with water; but ye shall be baptized with the Holy Ghost not many days hence.

_____ 3. Deuteronomy 1:45 And ye returned and wept before the Lord; but the Lord would not hearken to your voice, nor give ear unto you.

_____ 4. 2 Kings 7:1 Then Elisha said, Hear ye the word of the Lord; Thus saith the Lord, To morrow about this time shall a measure of fine flour be sold for a shekel, and two measures of barley for a shekel, in the gate of Samaria.

_____ 5. Exodus 20:25 And if thou wilt make me an altar of stone, thou shalt not build it of hewn stone: for if thou lift up thy tool upon it, thou hast polluted it.

_____ 6. Ruth 2:12 The Lord recompense thy work, and a full reward be given thee of the Lord God of Israel, under whose wings thou art come to trust.

_____ 7. Philippians 1:26 That your rejoicing may be more abundant in Jesus Christ for me by my coming to you again.

_____ 8. 2 Chronicles 19:3 Nevertheless there are good things found in thee, in that thou hast taken away the groves out of the land, and hast prepared thine heart to seek God.

_____ 9. Jeremiah 1:19 And they shall fight against thee; but they shall not prevail against thee; for I am with thee, saith the Lord, to deliver thee.

_____ 10. Leviticus 11:45 For I am the Lord that bringeth you up out of the land of Egypt, to be your God: ye shall therefore be holy, for I am holy.

_____ 11. Matthew 18:9 And if thine eye offend thee, pluck it out, and cast it from thee: it is better for thee to enter into life with one eye, rather than having two eyes to be cast into hell fire.

_____ 12. Judges 6:10 And I said unto you, I am the Lord your God; fear not the gods of the Amorites, in whose land ye dwell: but ye have not obeyed my voice.

_____ 13. John 3:5 Jesus answered, Verily, verily, I say unto thee, Except a man be born of water and of the Spirit, he cannot enter into the kingdom of God.

Synonym Scramble 1

Each set of scrambled words has a common meaning.
Use the definition as a hint.

Solution p. 126

To surround

EGBISEE = _ _ _ _ _ _ _ _ _ _ SEBET = _ _ _ _ _ _ _ _ _ _

AOSSMPC = _ _ _ _ _ _ _ _ _ _ SOLICNE = _ _ _ _ _ _ _ _ _ _

To punish

NCETASH = _ _ _ _ _ _ _ _ _ _ ITASHCES = _ _ _ _ _ _ _ _ _ _

RTRECOC = _ _ _ _ _ _ _ _ _ _ IFACFLT = _ _ _ _ _ _ _ _ _ _

To set free

RONMSA = _ _ _ _ _ _ _ _ _ _ MREEDE = _ _ _ _ _ _ _ _ _ _

DVELEIR = _ _ _ _ _ _ _ _ _ _ ERCSEU = _ _ _ _ _ _ _ _ _ _

To defeat

BUSUDE = _ _ _ _ _ _ _ _ _ _ SIFICODMT = _ _ _ _ _ _ _ _ _ _

EIRLPVA = _ _ _ _ _ _ _ _ _ _ ROENCQU = _ _ _ _ _ _ _ _ _ _

Clothing

ERGANMT = _ _ _ _ _ _ _ _ _ _ RAMIETN = _ _ _ _ _ _ _ _ _ _

VRTSEUE = _ _ _ _ _ _ _ _ _ _ TTEMNSEV = _ _ _ _ _ _ _ _ _ _

To follow advice

EDHE = _ _ _ _ _ _ _ _ _ _ TTANDE = _ _ _ _ _ _ _ _ _ _

GDEARR = _ _ _ _ _ _ _ _ _ _ AHNEKRE = _ _ _ _ _ _ _ _ _ _

Caterpillars #1

Use the definitions to place words from the word bank into each caterpillar. The letter at the end of one word will be the starting letter of the next word. Words may run across, up or down, but not backwards.

Solution p. 132

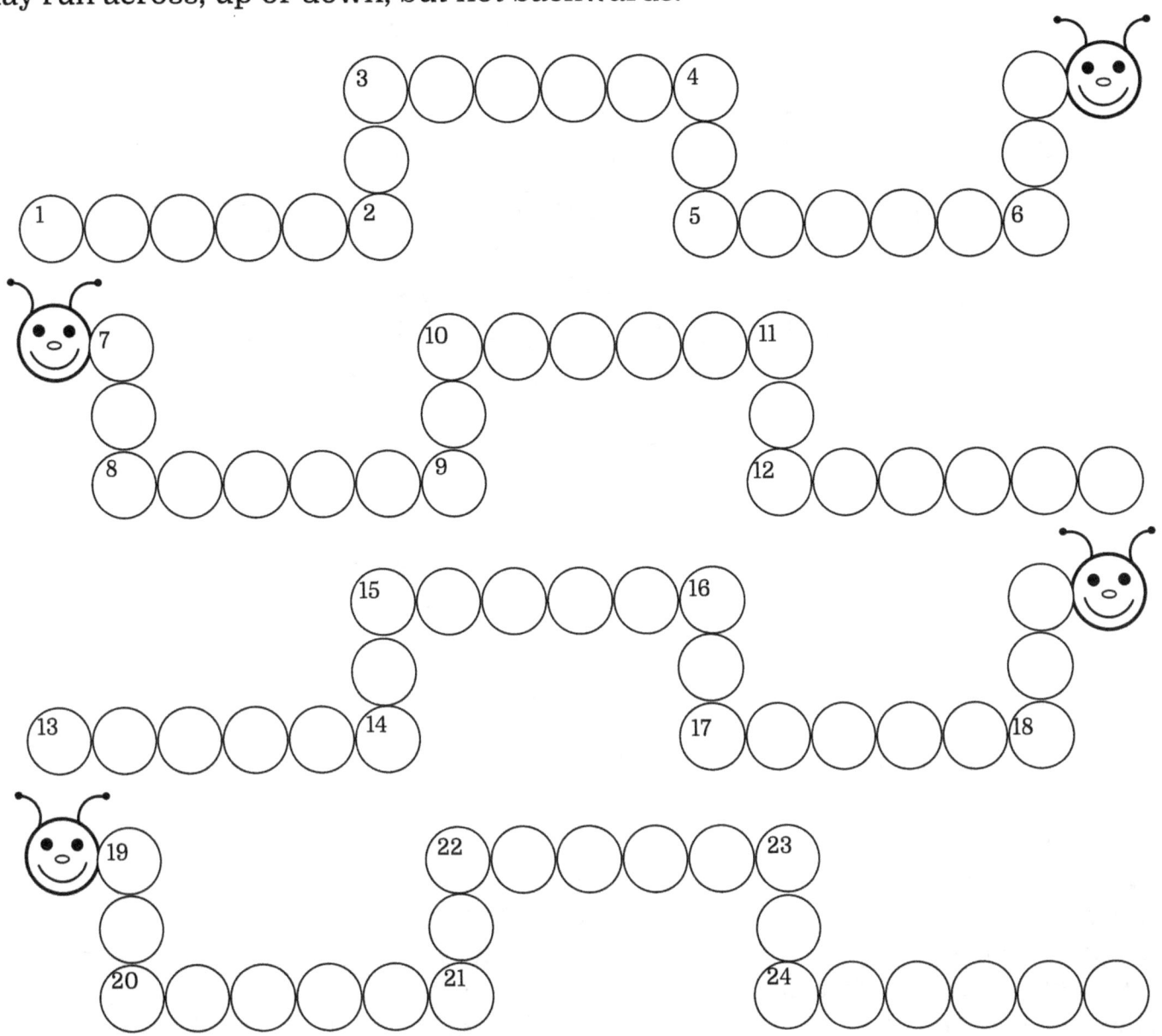

1. Moral excellence
2. Before
3. Castrated male
4. To cut or chop
5. To roll one's body on the ground
6. To become
7. Fuss
8. Hateful
9. Food dipped in liquid
10. To die
11. Chance
12. To follow after

13. Long narrow trench
14. Misery
15. To flee from, to shun
16. To know
17. Crowd
18. Trap
19. Iota
20. Twisted
21. Mother animal
22. Wonder
23. To hinder
24. A minute part

ADO   ODIOUS
DAM   PERISH
ERE   PURSUE
ESCHEW   SOP
EUNUCH   THRONG
FURROW   TITTLE
GIN   TWINED
HAP   VIRTUE
HEW   WALLOW
JOT   WOE
LET   WOT
MARVEL   WAX

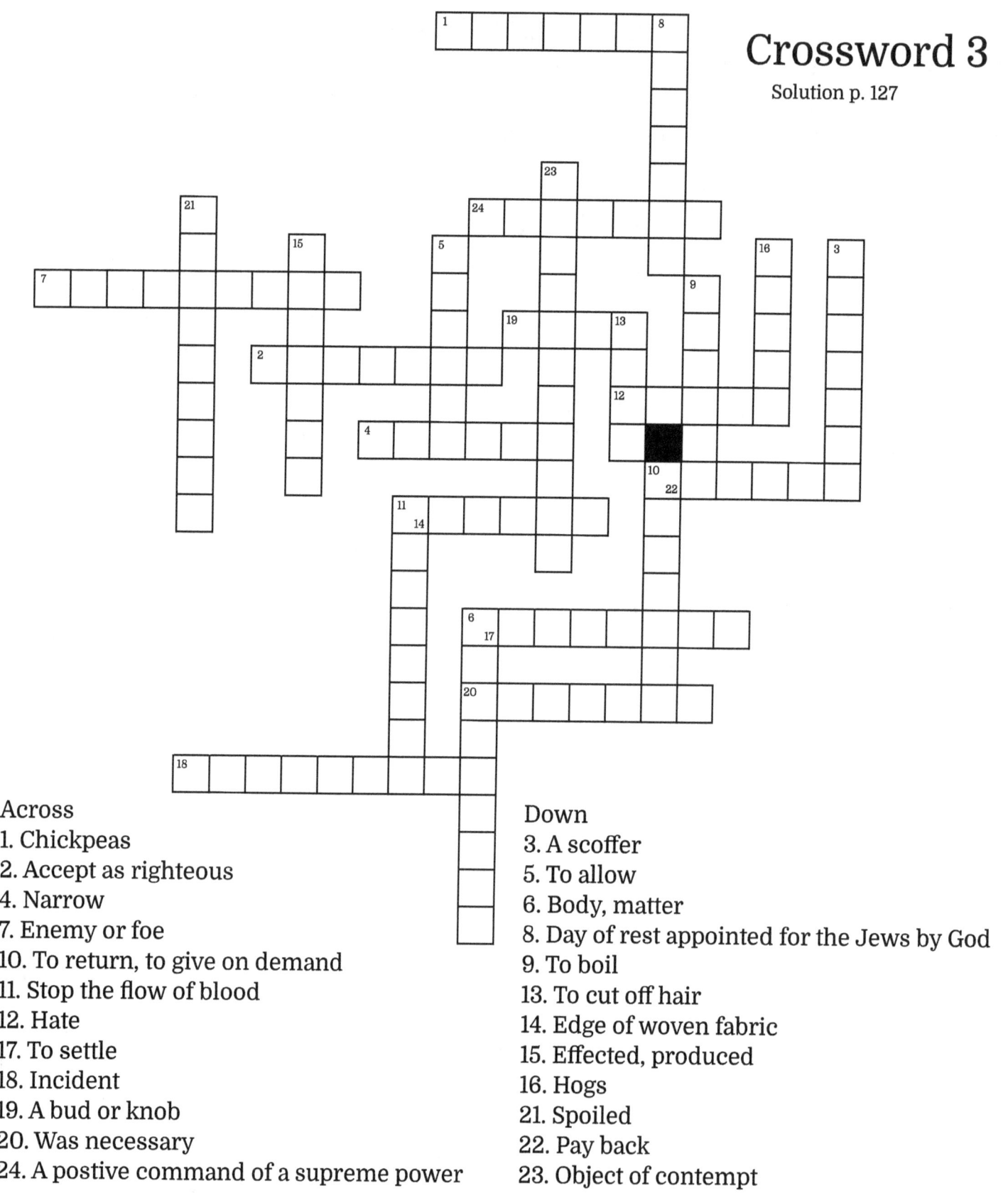

Crossword 3

Solution p. 127

Across

1. Chickpeas
2. Accept as righteous
4. Narrow
7. Enemy or foe
10. To return, to give on demand
11. Stop the flow of blood
12. Hate
17. To settle
18. Incident
19. A bud or knob
20. Was necessary
24. A postive command of a supreme power

Down

3. A scoffer
5. To allow
6. Body, matter
8. Day of rest appointed for the Jews by God
9. To boil
13. To cut off hair
14. Edge of woven fabric
15. Effected, produced
16. Hogs
21. Spoiled
22. Pay back
23. Object of contempt

WORD BANK	ADVERSARY	KNOP	SABBATH	STATUTE
	BEHOVED	LOTHE	SCORNER	STRAIT
	CORRUPTED	OCCURRENT	SEETHE	SUBSTANCE
	FITCHES	POLL	SELVEDGE	SUFFER
	GAZINGSTOCK	RENDER	STABLISH	SWINE
	JUSTIFY	REQUITE	STANCH	WROUGHT

A to Z #1

The answer to each lettered clue will contain its corresponding letter **somewhere** in the word. Select carefully from the word bank!

A. Wonder
B. Loud or violent
C. Religious rite for Jewish males
D. To ordain beforehand
E. Set deep and firm
F. Fondly
G. With steady application and care
H. Advancement
I. Unchangeableness
J. Hurtful to the rights of another
K. Blood relatives
L. To supply with light or knowledge
M. Despicable
N. Without restraint
O. Having the same or similar manner
P. Atoning sacrifice
Q. Feastings
R. Making new
S. Firmness of mind
T. Persistent request
U. Arguments
V. Changeableness
W. Any person without exception
X. In a very great degree
Y. Body of elders in the church
Z. The devil

Word Bank

ADMIRATION	ILLUMINATE
AFFECTIONATELY	IMMUTABILITY
BANQUETINGS	IMPORTUNITY
BEELZEBUB	INCONTINENT
BOISTEROUS	INJURIOUS
CIRCUMCISION	KINDRED
CONFORMABLE	PREDESTINATE
CONTEMPTIBLE	PRESBYTERY
DILIGENTLY	PROPITIATION
DISPUTINGS	REGENERATION
ENGRAFTED	STEDFASTNESS
EXCEEDING	VARIABLENESS
FURTHERANCE	WHOMSOEVER

A _____
B _____
C _____
D _____
E _____
F _____
G _____
H _____
I _____
J _____
K _____
L _____
M _____
N _____
O _____
P _____
Q _____
R _____
S _____
T _____
U _____
V _____
W _____
X _____
Y _____
Z _____

Common Denominator #1

Each of the answers to the following clues is made up of three segments (NOT syllables). The words have one segment in common which is in its correct position. Choose the others from the box and write them in the spaces provided.

Solution p. 132

	Beginning	Middle	End
1. A small piece of food	_____	**OR** ____	_____
2. Deserving	_____	**OR** ____	_____
3. Disagreement	_____	**OR** ____	_____
4. Collector of tax or duty	_____	_____	__**OR**___
5. Abandon	_____	**OR** ____	_____
6. Strengthen	_____	**OR** ____	_____
7. A scoffer, a despiser	_____	___**OR**___	_____
8. Distinguished persons	_____	___**OR**___	_____
9. Character	_____	_____	__**OR**__
10. Powerful	_____	___**OR**___	_____
11. Of lower place	_____	_____	__**OR**__
12. One who attempts to reconcile opposing parties	_____	_____	__**OR**__
13. To pledge an estate as security for money lent	_____	**OR** ____	_____
14. A person born outside the country	_____	___**OR**___	_____
15. Lack of knowledge	_____	___**OR**___	_____

SEGMENTS

ACT	EN	FERI	MED	TGAGE
ANCE	EX	IAT	NER	THIES
CIBLE	F	IGN	SAKE	THY
D	F	IN	SC	TIFY
DISC	F	M	SEL	W
EIGNER	F	M	T	W

Which Word?

Which of the words with similar meaning belongs in each verse? Circle your answer. Check your answers in your Bible.

Ezekiel 20:16
Because they despised my judgments, and walked not in my statutes, but
_____my sabbaths: for their heart went after their idols.

Corrupted	Defiled	Polluted

1 Corinthians 1:27
But God hath chosen the foolish things of the world to confound the_____;
and God hath chosen the weak things of the world to confound the things which are
mighty;

Circumspect	Prudent	Wise

Romans 8:1
There is therefore now no _____ to them which are in Christ Jesus, who walk
not after the flesh, but after the Spirit.

Condemnation	Damnation	Perdition

Luke 21:4
For all these have of their abundance cast in unto the offerings of God: but she of her
_____ hath cast in all the living that she had.

Penury	Poverty	Want

Matthew 5:11
Blessed are ye, when men shall _____ you, and persecute you, and shall
say all manner of evil against you falsely, for my sake.

Deride	Rail	Revile

Isaiah 26:5
For he bringeth down them that dwell on high; the _____ city, he layeth it low;
he layeth it low, even to the ground; he bringeth it even to the dust.

Stately	Eminent	Lofty

Ruth 2:15
And when she was risen up to glean, Boaz commanded his young men, saying, Let
her glean even among the sheaves, and _____ her not:

Reproach	Reprove	Upbraid

Jonah 1:15
So they took up Jonah, and cast him forth into the sea: and the sea _____ from her
raging.

Ceased	Halted	Stayed

Fill in the Blank - 1 Peter Chapter 3

Use the definitions in parentheses to select the words that belong in the text and write them in the blanks. Check your answers in your Bible.

3 Likewise, ye wives, be in (yielding to power)_____ to your own husbands; that, if any obey not the word, they also may without the word be won by the (general behavior) _____ of the wives; 2 While they (observe) _____ your chaste conversation coupled with fear. 3 Whose adorning let it not be that outward adorning of (braiding) _____ the hair, and of wearing of gold, or of putting on of (clothing) _____; 4 But let it be the hidden man of the heart, in that which is not (subject to decay) _____, even the ornament of a meek and quiet spirit, which is in the sight of God of great price. 5 For after this manner in the old time the holy women also, who trusted in God, (decorated) _____ themselves, being in subjection unto their own husbands: 6 Even as Sara obeyed Abraham, calling him lord: whose daughters ye are, as long as ye do well, and are not afraid with any (fear) _____. 7 Likewise, ye husbands, dwell with them according to knowledge, giving honour unto the wife, as unto the weaker vessel, and as being heirs together of the grace of life; that your prayers be not (prevented from moving forward) _____. 8 Finally, be ye all of one mind, having (sympathy) _____ one of another, love as brethren, be pitiful, be (polite) _____: 9 Not (returning) _____ evil for evil, or railing for railing: but (on the other hand) _____ blessing; knowing that ye are thereunto called, that ye should inherit a blessing. 10 For he that will love life, and see good days, let him (hold back) _____ his tongue from evil, and his lips that they speak no guile: 11 Let him (flee from) _____ evil, and do good; let him seek peace, and (follow) _____ it. 12 For the eyes of the Lord are over the righteous, and his ears are open unto their prayers: but the face of the Lord is against them that do evil.

ADORNED
AMAZEMENT
APPAREL
BEHOLD
COMPASSION
CONTRARIWISE

CONVERSATION
CORRUPTIBLE
COURTEOUS
ENSUE
ESCHEW
HINDERED

PLAITING
REFRAIN
RENDERING
SUBJECTION

Down the Stairs #1

Use the definitions to place words from the word bank into each row. One letter is given in each word. One word will be used twice.   Solution p. 122

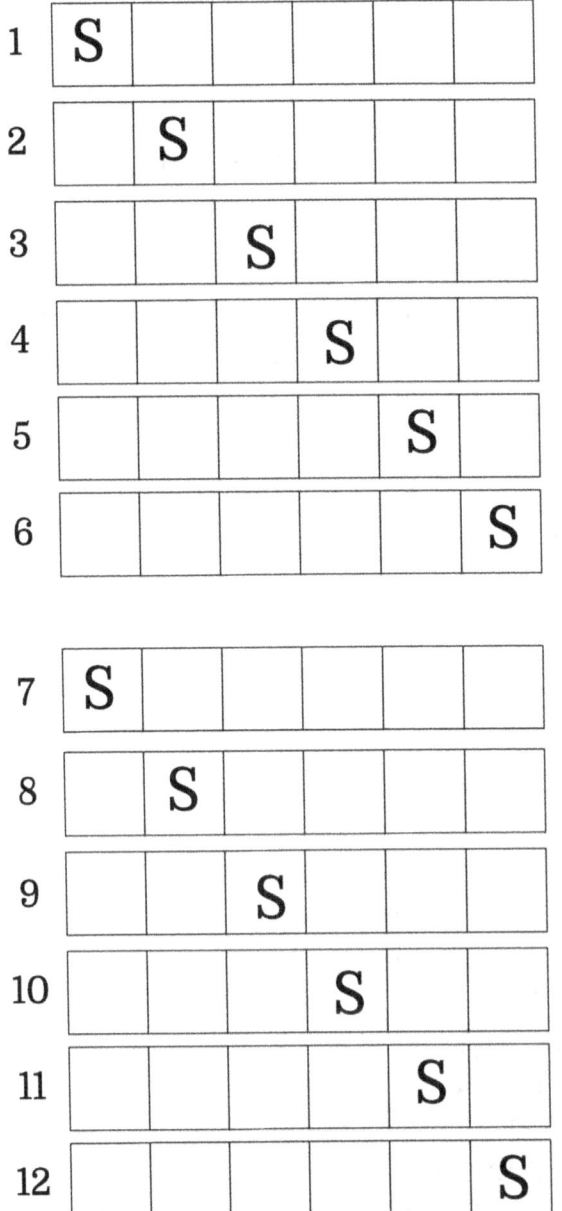

Word Bank

ASTRAY
CHASTE
CUSTOM
DAMSEL
DESERT
DROPSY
ESTATE
ESTEEM
FAMISH
HEDGES
NOISED
OPPOSE
OUCHES
PSALMS
SAVOUR
SEEMLY
SOUGHT
STOCKS
TACHES
VANISH
VESSEL
VISAGE
WHELPS

1. Taste or odor
2. Condition of any person or thing
3. Face
4. Container
5. Watery swelling in the body
6. Settings for gemstones
7. Searched for
8. Out of the right way
9. Uninhabited
10. Young woman
11. To nearly die from hunger or thirst
12. Young of an animal

13. Proper, appropriate
14. To value
15. Tax or tribute
16. Reported
17. Disappear
18. Catches or buttons
19. Punishment device
20. Sacred songs
21. Common practice
22. Pure
23. To act against
24. Thicket

Crossword 4

Solution p. 127

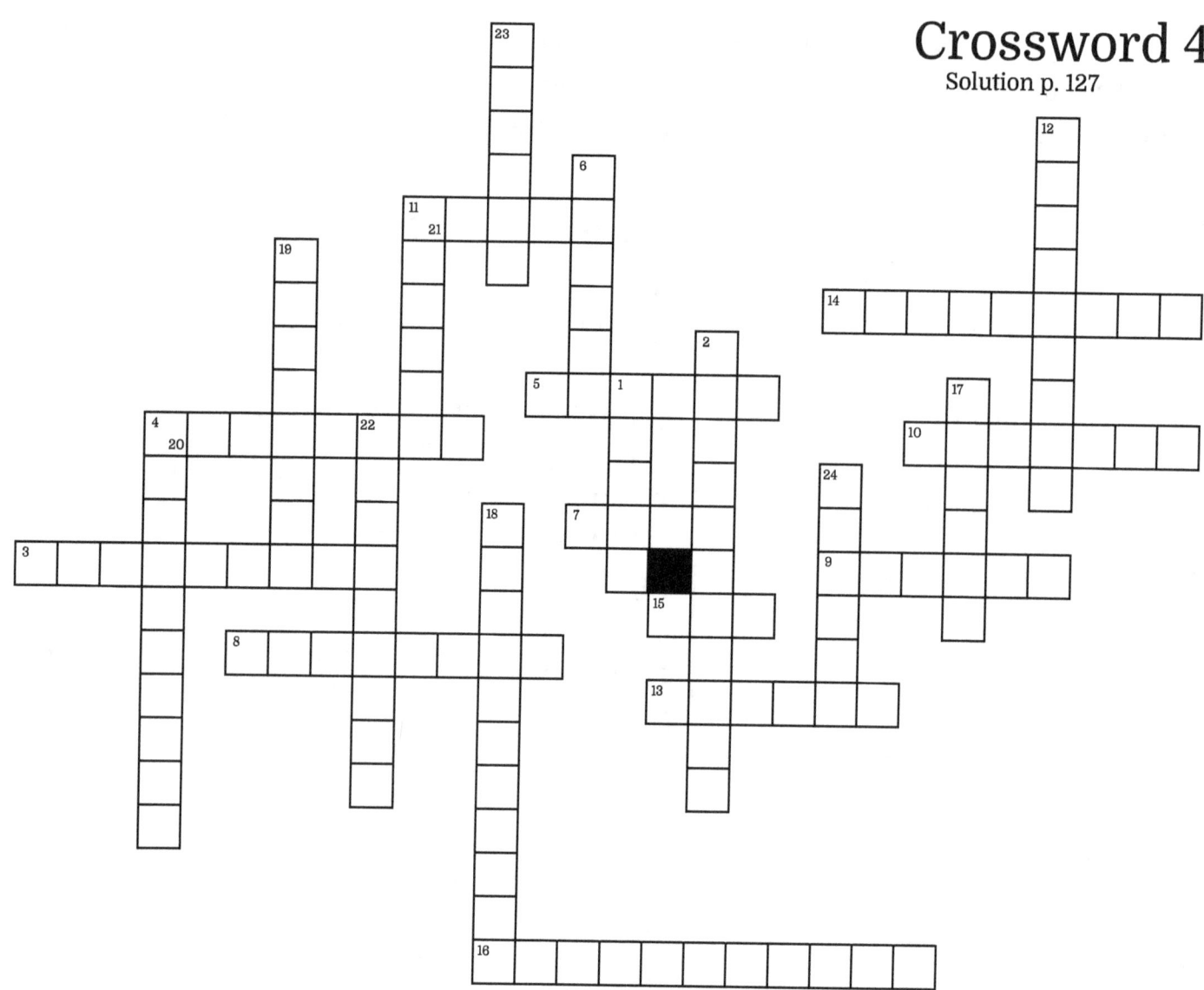

Across

3. Place where grapes are squeezed
5. To place
7. Manner
8. Shame, disgrace
9. Reject the authority of a ruler
10. A poisonous plant
11. Anything troublesome
13. A young woman
14. Utter destruction
15. To cut or chop
16. Moveable building
20. A scale

Down

1. Killed
2. Contract between people or states
4. One who confers a benefit
6. Bear
12. Unchangeable
17. Make a sign to another
18. Cautious
19. Deliverance
21. From that place
22. To compel or force
23. A long narrow trench
24. To put forth effort

WORD BANK

BALANCES	CONSTRAIN	IMMUTABLE	STRIVE
BECKON	DAMSEL	PERDITION	TABERNACLES
BENEFACTOR	ENDURE	REPROACH	THENCE
BESTOW	FURROW	REVOLT	THORN
CIRCUMSPECT	HEMLOCK	RIDDANCE	WINEPRESS
CONFEDERACY	HEW	SLAIN	WISE

Daisy Chain #1

Beginning at #1 and moving clockwise around the petals, fill in a word from the word bank that matches each definition. Within each flower, the last letter of each answer will also be the first letter of the next answer.

Solution on p. 132

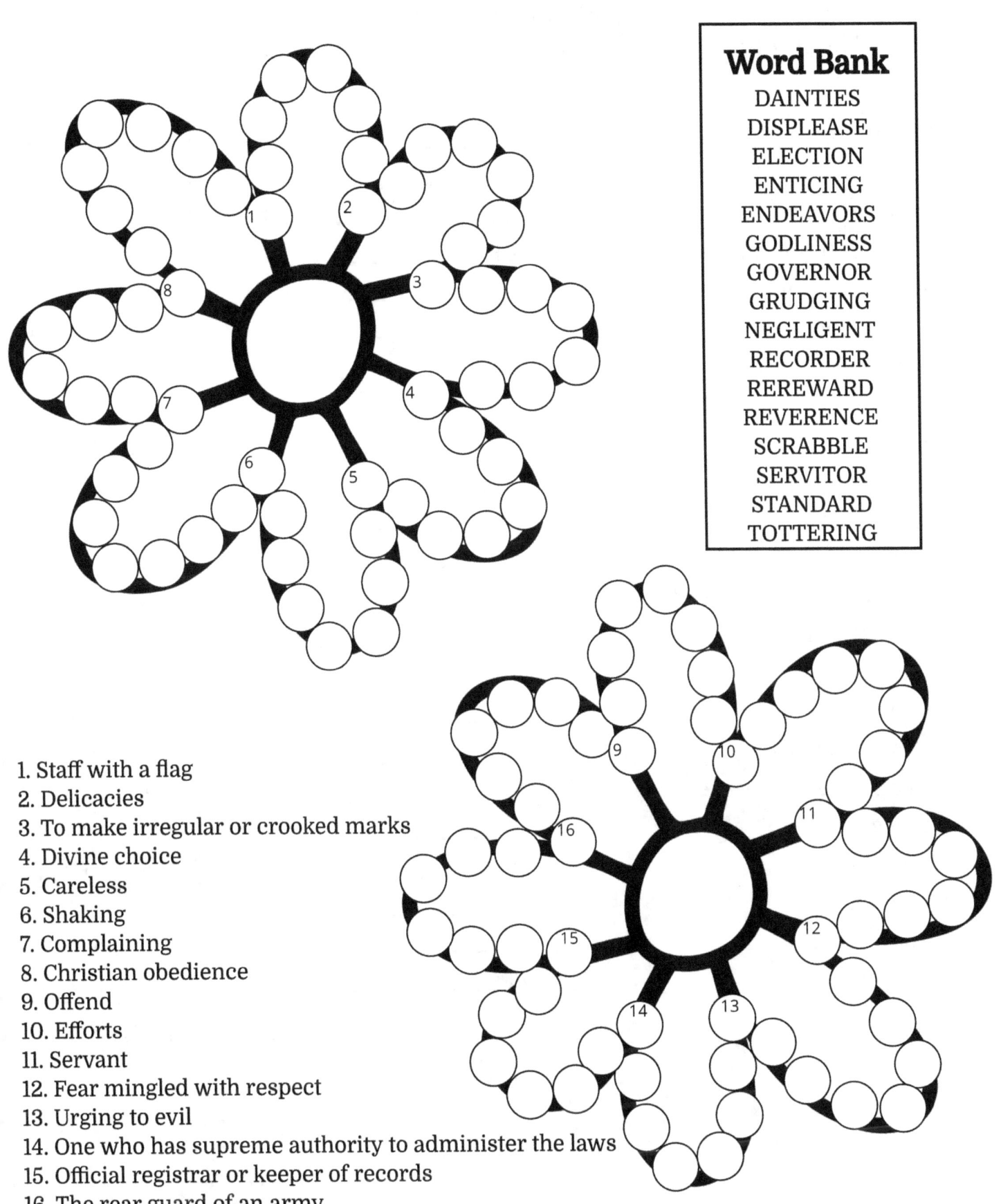

Word Bank

DAINTIES
DISPLEASE
ELECTION
ENTICING
ENDEAVORS
GODLINESS
GOVERNOR
GRUDGING
NEGLIGENT
RECORDER
REREWARD
REVERENCE
SCRABBLE
SERVITOR
STANDARD
TOTTERING

1. Staff with a flag
2. Delicacies
3. To make irregular or crooked marks
4. Divine choice
5. Careless
6. Shaking
7. Complaining
8. Christian obedience
9. Offend
10. Efforts
11. Servant
12. Fear mingled with respect
13. Urging to evil
14. One who has supreme authority to administer the laws
15. Official registrar or keeper of records
16. The rear guard of an army

23

Finish the Word #2

The following verbs have the same beginning. Can you finish them, using the definitions and word lists?
The number of blanks indicates the number of missing letters.

To delay	DE _ _ _	
To eat up	DE _ _ _ _	
To depart from life	DE _ _ _ _ _	
To depart from paths of right	DE _ _ _ _ _	
To cause to believe a lie	DE _ _ _ _ _	
To pass from one to another	DE _ _ _ _ _	
To cheat	DE _ _ _ _ _	

DECEASE
DECEIVE
DECLINE
DEFER
DEFRAUD
DELIVER
DEVOUR

To see the difference between things	DI _ _ _ _ _
To think unworthy	DI _ _ _ _ _
To make uneasy or restless	DI _ _ _ _ _ _
To make void	DI _ _ _ _ _ _
To assume a false appearance	DI _ _ _ _ _ _ _
To worsen the appearance of	DI _ _ _ _ _ _ _

DISANNUL
DISCERN
DISDAIN
DISFIGURE
DISQUIET
DISSEMBLE

To advance	PR _ _ _ _ _
To call to action	PR _ _ _ _ _
To go before, to precede	PR _ _ _ _ _
To lengthen	PR _ _ _ _
To obtain	PR _ _ _ _
To succeed	PR _ _ _ _ _
To announce	PR _ _ _ _ _ _
To predict	PR _ _ _ _ _ _

PREVENT
PROCLAIM
PROCURE
PROLONG
PROMOTE
PROPHESY
PROSPER
PROVOKE

Solution p. 120

Secret Word #2

Solution p. 124

Place a word from the box below on each line. The circled letters in each puzzle will spell out a secret word also found in the box (and in the Bible).

To reproach

Support

A bond of connection

Count

Secret Word: _____

Symbol of power

To build or erect

Uproar

To tear or split

Secret Word: _____

To choose

To cut off hair

Scattered, as seed

To love excessively

Secret Word: _____

Valley

Remove from milk

To make known

Walked

Secret Word: _____

To clothe ornately

Wearing shoes

Despicable

Muddy

Secret Word: _____

Charity for the poor

Suitable

Type of large grass

Near

Secret Word: _____

ALMS	LAKE	NIGH	REND	TELL
AMEN	LAST	POLL	RIOT	TROD
DECK	LIST	RAIL	SHEW	VALE
DOER	LOST	RAIN	SHOD	VILE
DOTE	MEET	REAR	SOWN	WEAN
HORN	MIRY	REED	STAY	YOKE

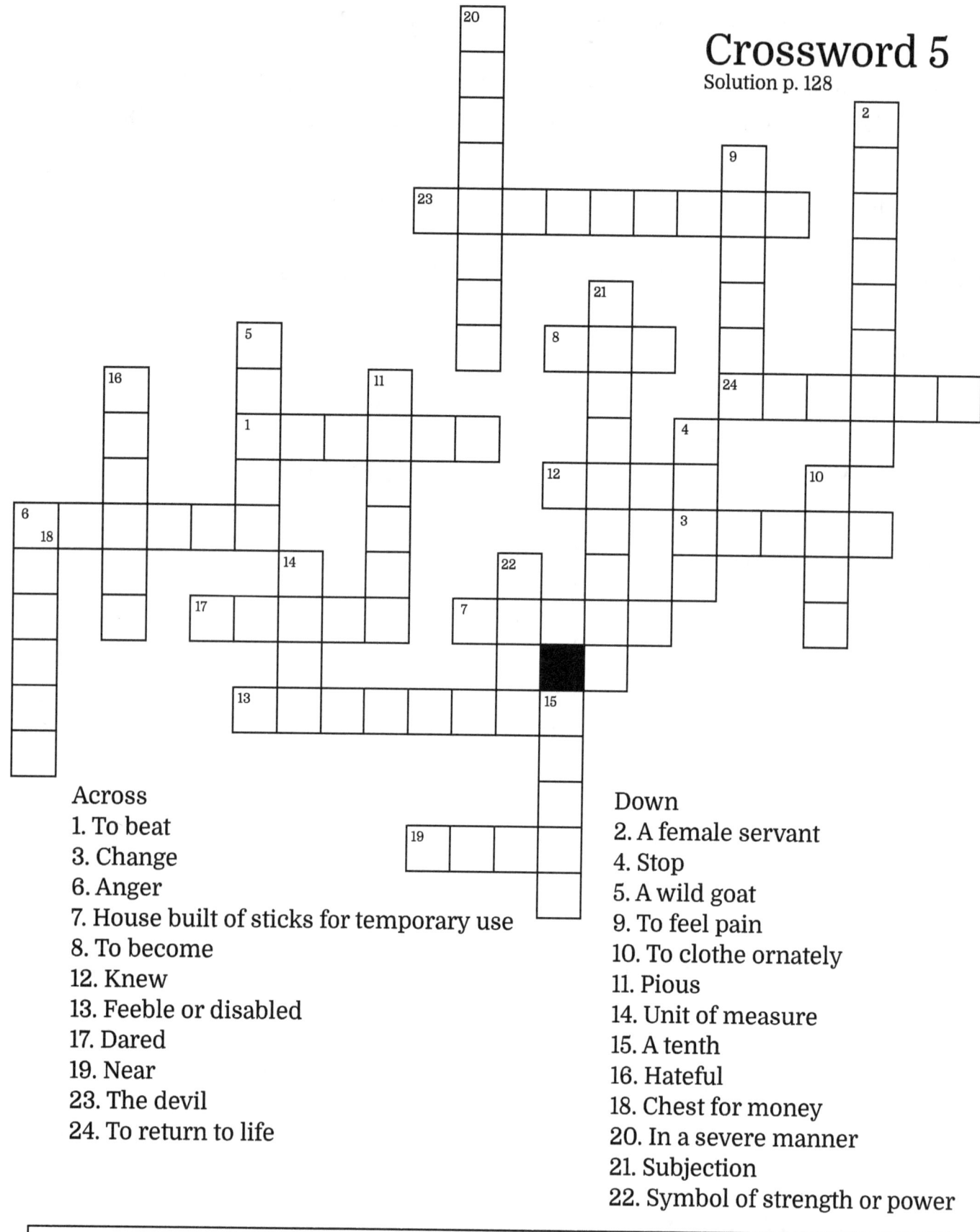

Crossword 5

Solution p. 128

Across
1. To beat
3. Change
6. Anger
7. House built of sticks for temporary use
8. To become
12. Knew
13. Feeble or disabled
17. Dared
19. Near
23. The devil
24. To return to life

Down
2. A female servant
4. Stop
5. A wild goat
9. To feel pain
10. To clothe ornately
11. Pious
14. Unit of measure
15. A tenth
16. Hateful
18. Chest for money
20. In a severe manner
21. Subjection
22. Symbol of strength or power

WORD BANK			
ALTER	COFFER	HORN	STAY
BEELZEBUB	DECK	IMPOTENT	SUFFER
BITTERLY	DEVOUT	NIGH	THRESH
BOOTH	DRAM	ODIOUS	TITHE
CAPTIVITY	DURST	REVIVE	WAX
CHOLER	HANDMAID	SATYR	WIST

Double Trouble #1

Place the correct set of missing double letters into each blank using the definitions as your guide. Some words will have more than one set of doubles.

1. One who indulges in excess eating   G L U _ _ O N
2. Seat   S E _ _ L E
3. An obscure path intersecting the main road   C R O _ _ W A Y
4. Day of rest appointed for the Jews by God   S A _ _ A T H
5. Order in lines   A _ _ A Y
6. Official orders   C O _ _ I _ _ I O N
7. Wall raised on a building   B A _ _ L E M E N T
8. Human carried transport vehicles   L I _ _ E R S
9. To be enough   S U _ _ I C E
10. Stuttering   S T A _ _ E R I N G
11. Aromatic and medicinal plant   M Y _ _ H
12. Sheath of a sword   S C A _ _ A R D
13. Soften   S U _ _ L E
14. To follow in order   S U _ _ _ _ D
15. Fatal disease among cattle   M U _ _ A I N
16. Preparing land for seed and keeping it weed free   T I _ _ A G E
17. Chains for the feet   F E _ _ E R S
18. To make a loud noise   B E _ _ O W
19. Vocal expression   U _ _ E R A N C E
20. The rod on a spinning wheel   D I S T A _ _
21. Skillful   C U _ _ I N G
22. Grieve or distress   A _ _ L I C T
23. To make less flexible   S T I _ _ E N
24. Resin used as perfume and medicine   B D E _ _ I U M
25. Embassy   A M B A _ _ A G E

LETTER BANK

BB	FF	LL	MM	RR	SS	TT
BB	FF	LL	NN	RR	TT	TT
CC	FF	LL	PP	SS	TT	TT
EE	FF	MM	RR	SS	TT	

Select-A-Syllable #2

Each of the answers to the following clues is made up of two syllables that can be found in the box. Put them together and write your completed words in the spaces provided. The numbers in parentheses indicate the total number of letters in each answer. Each syllable will be used only once.   Solution p. 121

1. Extreme (5)   _____

2. To be unsettled in opinion (5)   _____

3. To lessen or diminish (5)   _____

4. Interior organs (6)   _____

5. Pious (6)   _____

6. Kind regard (6)   _____

7. Type or representation (6)   _____

8. To go up (6)   _____

9. Prickly shrub (7)   _____

10. A private room (7)   _____

11. Agreement (7)   _____

12. To do something that is expected (7)   _____

13. Fastener for a shoe (7)   _____

14. Waste material (7)   _____

15. To have power over (7)   _____

16. Talking without meaning (7)   _____

17. To make known (7)   _____

18. A mound of earth used for defense of a place (7) _____

19. Pertaining to a servant (7)   _____

20. Struck (7)   _____

Syllable Box

A	CEND	FIG	PRAT	TEN
AS	CHAM	FILL	PUB	TER
BATE	CON	FUL	RAM	URE
BER	DE	ING	RUB	UT
BISH	ELS	LATCH	SENT	VILE
BLE	ER	LISH	SER	VOUR
BOW	ET	PART	SESS	VOUT
BRAM	FA	POS	SMIT	WAV

28

M_ss_ng V_w_ls

#1

(Missing Vowels) Fill in the missing vowels to form some commonly used adverbs. You will notice that the same meaning may apply to more than one word.

Solution p. 122

From what place	wh _ nc _
For which reason, why	wh _ r _ f _ r _
Also	l _ k _ w _ s _
From this or that	th _ r _ fr _ m
With that or this	th _ r _ w _ th
Gladly	f _ _ n
Nevertheless	h _ wb _ _ t
In which	wh _ r _ _ n
By that	th _ r _ b _
On which or on what	wh _ r _ _ n
Besides	m _ r _ _ v _ r
To what place	wh _ th _ r
From this time forward	h _ nc _ f _ rw _ rd
Near	n _ gh
In whatever	wh _ r _ _ ns _ _ v _ r
In some future time	h _ r _ _ ft _ r
Frequently	_ ft _ nt _ m _ s
At the same time	w _ th _ l
As much as	_ n _ sm _ ch
In fact	wh _ r _ _ s
From this time forward	h _ nc _ f _ rth
Up to this time or place	h _ th _ rt _
Of that or this	th _ r _ _ f
By chance, perhaps	p _ r _ dv _ nt _ r _
In time past	_ f _ r _ t _ m _
With which	wh _ r _ w _ th
Of what or of which	wh _ r _ _ f
Out of that or this	th _ r _ _ _ t
To that place	th _ th _ r

Picture Match #1- Animals

Each of the following verses contains the name of an animal in ALL CAPS. Use the letters on the pictures to match the verse to the correct animal. One animal will be used twice.

Solution p. 125

A   B   C   D

E   F   G   H

I   J   K   L

M   N   O   P

1. _ _ _ _ _   Song of Solomon 2:9
   My beloved is like a roe or a young HART: behold, he standeth behind our wall, he looketh forth at the windows, shewing himself through the lattice.

2. _ _ _ _ _   Revelation 9:10
   And they had tails like unto SCORPIONs, and there were stings in their tails: and their power was to hurt men five months.

3. _ _ _ _ _   Numbers 23:22
   God brought them out of Egypt; he hath as it were the strength of an UNICORN.

4. _ _ _ _ _ Genesis 8:7
And he sent forth a RAVEN, which went forth to and fro, until the waters were dried up from off the earth.

5. _ _ _ _ _ Deuteronomy 28:4
Blessed shall be the fruit of thy body, and the fruit of thy ground, and the fruit of thy cattle, the increase of thy KINE, and the flocks of thy sheep.

6. _ _ _ _ _ Jeremiah 14:5
Yea, the HIND also calved in the field, and forsook it, because there was no grass.

7. _ _ _ _ _ John 12:15
Fear not, daughter of Sion: behold, thy King cometh, sitting on an ASS's colt.

8. _ _ _ _ _ Isaiah 34:11
But the cormorant and the BITTERN shall possess it; the owl also and the raven shall dwell in it: and he shall stretch out upon it the line of confusion, and the stones of emptiness.

9. _ _ _ _ _ Deuteronomy 14:7
Nevertheless these ye shall not eat of them that chew the cud, or of them that divide the cloven hoof; as the camel, and the hare, and the CONEY: for they chew the cud, but divide not the hoof; therefore they are unclean unto you.

10. _ _ _ _ _ Job 40:15
Behold now BEHEMOTH, which I made with thee; he eateth grass as an ox.

11. _ _ _ _ _ Matthew 10:31
Fear ye not therefore, ye are of more value than many SPARROWs.

12. _ _ _ _ _ Jeremiah 2:23
How canst thou say, I am not polluted, I have not gone after Baalim? see thy way in the valley, know what thou hast done: thou art a swift DROMEDARY traversing her ways.

13. _ _ _ _ _ Exodus 29:12
And thou shalt take of the blood of the BULLOCK, and put it upon the horns of the altar with thy finger, and pour all the blood beside the bottom of the altar.

14. _ _ _ _ _ Jeremiah 8:7
Yea, the stork in the heaven knoweth her appointed times; and the TURTLE and the crane and the swallow observe the time of their coming; but my people know not the judgment of the Lord.

15. _ _ _ _ _ Romans 3:13
Their throat is an open sepulchre; with their tongues they have used deceit; the poison of ASPs is under their lips:

16. _ _ _ _ _ Deuteronomy 28:42
All thy trees and fruit of thy land shall the LOCUST consume.

17. _ _ _ _ _ Genesis 8:9
But the DOVE found no rest for the sole of her foot, and she returned unto him into the ark, for the waters were on the face of the whole earth: then he put forth his hand, and took her, and pulled her in unto him into the ark.

Crossword 6

Solution p. 128

Across
3. Bravery
6. To rescue or free
7. One who is taken against their will
10. To beat
11. One who pretends to be what he is not
12. To repay, payback
16. To frighten
17. Household deities
19. A section of a place
20. Investigation, examination
23. Discern
24. Thicket

Down
1. Wetland plants
2. Cloak
4. Charity for the poor
5. Expression of sorrow
8. Disappear
9. To make known
13. Loud or violent
14. Part
15. A type of shield
18. Clothing
21. Put to death by means of a cross
22. Trouble

WORD BANK	ALMS	CRUCIFY	HYPOCRITE	QUARTER
	BOISTEROUS	CUMBER	INQUISITION	RECOMPENCE
	BRAY	DELIVER	LAMENTATION	TELL
	BUCKLER	FRAY	MANTLE	TERAPHIM
	BULRUSHES	GARMENT	PORTION	VALOUR
	CAPTIVE	HEDGES	PUBLISH	VANISH

Compound Words #1

Match the two parts of each compound word using the definition. Write the letter of the second half in the blank space following the first half.   Solution p. 123

1.	Falling from faith into sin =	BACK	+ _____	A. BIBBER
2.	Slavery =	BOND	+ _____	B. BRAND
3.	Pest destructive to trees or plants =	CANKER	+ _____	C. BREAD
4.	A heap of manure =	DUNG	+ _____	D. BREAKERS
5.	Evening =	EVEN	+ _____	E. CLOTH
6.	Eternal, perpetual =	EVER	+ _____	F. FARING
7.	Piece of flaming wood =	FIRE	+ _____	G. FAST
8.	The foremost part =	FORE	+ _____	H. FLOOR
9.	Quadruple =	FOUR	+ _____	I. FOLD
10.	A female servant =	HAND	+ _____	J. FOLK
11.	Farmer =	HUSBAND	+ _____	K. FRONT
12.	Small container used to hold ink =	INK	+ _____	L. GLORY
13.	Persons of the same family =	KINS	+ _____	M. HILL
14.	Hard surface used to grind grain =	MILL	+ _____	N. HORN
15.	Ruin =	OVER	+ _____	O. HOUSE
16.	A piece of a broken pot =	POT	+ _____	P. LASTING
17.	Having circular lines on the body =	RING	+ _____	Q. MAID
18.	Coarse garment worn for mourning =	SACK	+ _____	R. MAN
19.	Hallowed loaves =	SHEW	+ _____	S. MEN
20.	A foreteller =	SOOTH	+ _____	T. SAYER
21.	Those armed with lances =	SPEAR	+ _____	U. SERVICE
22.	Firm, constant =	STED	+ _____	V. SHERD
23.	Building for keeping goods =	STORE	+ _____	W. SLIDING
24.	An area where grain is beat out =	THRESHING	+ _____	X. STAND
25.	Those who violate covenants =	TRUCE	+ _____	Y. STONE
26.	Empty pride =	VAIN	+ _____	Z. STRAKED
27.	A planting of grapevines =	VINE	+ _____	AA. THROW
28.	On a journey =	WAY	+ _____	BB. TIDE
29.	A great drinker =	WINE	+ _____	CC. WORM
30.	To resist =	WITH	+ _____	DD. YARD

Anagrams #2

Each word set is an anagram of a single Bible word. Use the definition to unscramble them. Stumped? Use the reference verse for help.   Solution p. 125

Example: Owing something to someone   bend diet   ___indebted__

1. Violation of sacred things (Romans 2:22)   graces lie   _____
2. Unnecessary (Leviticus 22:23)   user fouls up   _____
3. Stupid or uncivilized (Proverbs 12:1)   brush it   _____
4. Likeness (Ezekiel 8:2)   an ape caper   _____
5. Set apart for the service of God (Exodus 30:30)   ocean crest   _____
6. A moveable building (Exodus 33:7)   bat cleaner   _____
7. To put an end to (Isaiah 2:8)   ash boil   _____
8. Armies (Romans 9:29)   has boat   _____
9. Interwoven (Exodus 28:24)   new earth   _____
10. To attribute (Romans 4:8)   time up   _____
11. Great misfortunes (Proverbs 17:5)   a claim site   _____
12. Supplied with light (Psalm 97:4)   needle thing   _____
13. Establishment (Philippians 1:7)   romantic info   _____
14. Distribution (Colossians 1:25)   aside inn stop   _____
15. Suspicions (1 Timothy 6:4)   rising sums   _____
16. An additional name (Matthew 10:3)   man user   _____
17. An animal ready for slaughter (1 Samuel 15:9)   flag tin   _____
18. To make unholy, pollute (Ezekiel 23:38)   open far   _____
19. Place set apart for worship (1 Chronicles 22:19)   scary aunt   _____
20. Preacher of the gospel (2 Timothy 4:5)   gave listen   _____
21. Those who speak evil of others (1 Timothy 3:11)   laser nerds   _____
22. Remote, lonely (Job 30:3)   rail toys   _____

Fill in the Blank from Acts 27:9-19

Use the definitions in parentheses to select the words that belong in the text and write them in the blanks. Check your answers in your Bible.

9 Now when much time was spent, and when sailing was now dangerous, because the (time of abstaining from food) _____was now already past, Paul (cautioned) _____ them, 10 And said unto them, Sirs, I (understand) _____that this voyage will be with hurt and much damage, not only of the (cargo) _____ and ship, but also of our lives. 11 Nevertheless the (commander of 100 soldiers) _____ believed the master and the owner of the ship, more than those things which were spoken by Paul. 12 And because the haven was not (suitable) _____to winter in, the more part advised to depart thence also, if by any means they might (arrive at) _____to Phenice, and there to winter; which is an (harbor) _____ of Crete, and lieth toward the south west and north west. 13 And when the south wind blew softly, supposing that they had obtained their purpose, loosing (from that place) _____, they sailed close by Crete. 14 But not long after there arose against it a (stormy) _____wind, called Euroclydon. 15 And when the ship was caught, and could not bear up into the wind, we let her drive. 16 And running under a certain island which is called Clauda, we had much work to come by the boat: 17 Which when they had taken up, they used helps, (binding below) _____the ship; and, fearing lest they should fall into the quicksands, strake sail, and so were driven. 18 And we being exceedingly tossed with a (violent storm) _____, the next day they (unloaded) _____the ship; 19 And the third day we cast out with our own hands the (rigging) _____of the ship.

ADMONISHED	HAVEN	TACKLING
ATTAIN	LADING	TEMPEST
CENTURION	LIGHTENED	TEMPESTUOUS
COMMODIOUS	PERCEIVE	THENCE
FAST	UNDERGIRDING	

Crossword 7

Solution p. 128

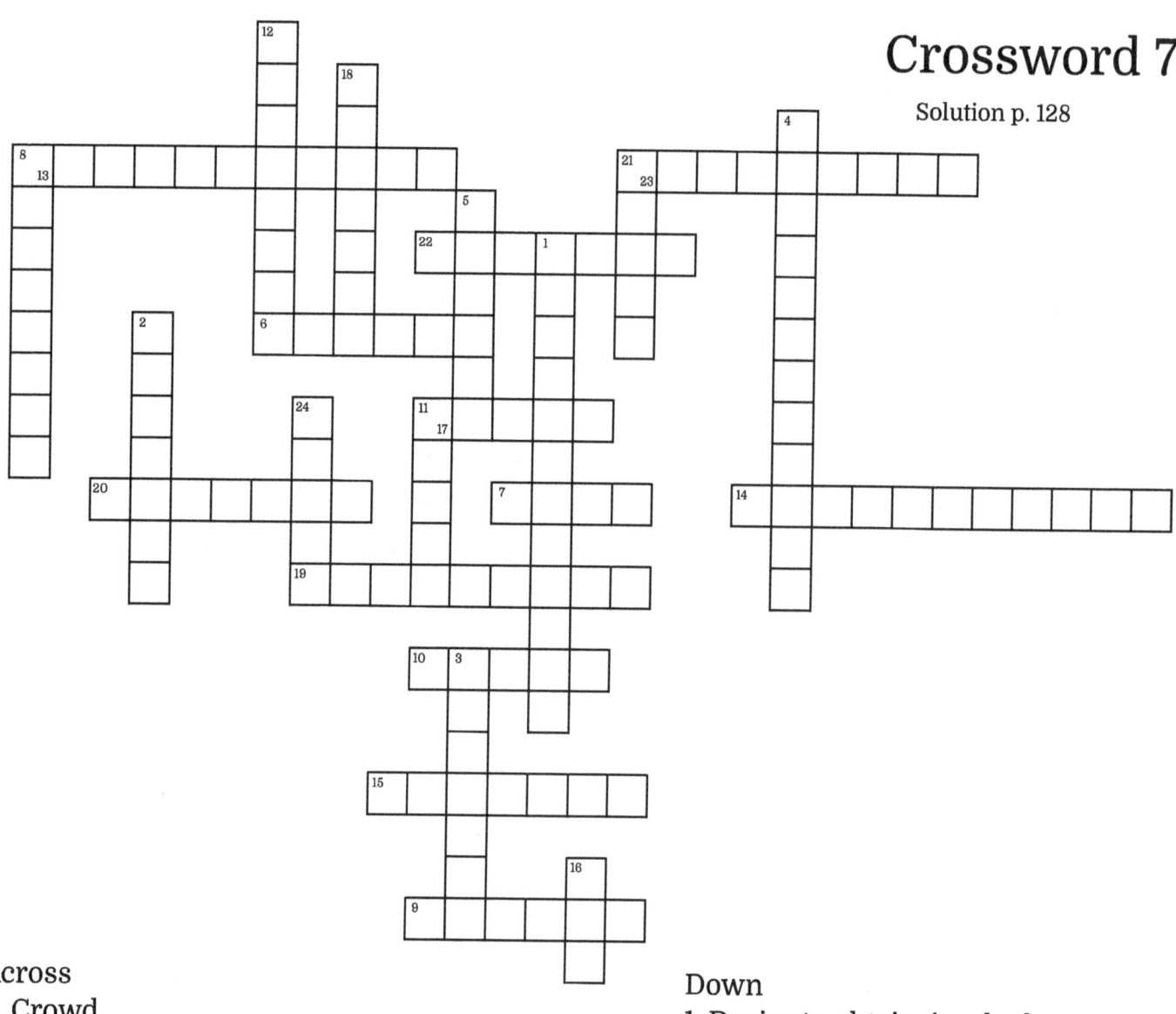

Across

6. Crowd
7. Rage, anger
9. Cut off the head
10. Middle
13. Object of extreme hatred
14. Argument or controversy
15. Stumps of grain left in the ground after reaping
17. Violent anger
19. Goods
20. Sure
22. String that fastens a shoe
23. Water raven

Down

1. Desire to obtain, in a bad sense
2. Entrust
3. Ask
4. General behavior
5. Feed trough
8. What idolatry is, spiritually
11. Goods for sale
12. Enjoyable
16. Chance
18. To what place
21. Crack or crevice
24. The inward parts, the heart

WORD BANK			
ABOMINATION	CONVERSATION	INQUIRE	STUBBLE
ADULTERY	CORMORANT	LATCHET	SUBSTANCE
BEHEAD	COVETOUSNESS	MANGER	THRONG
CERTAIN	DISPUTATION	MIDST	WARES
CLEFT	FURY	PLEASANT	WHITHER
COMMEND	HAP	REINS	WRATH

Sort Them Out #1

Write each word under the correct category. Each answer will be used only once.

Solution p. 120

Shekel Maneh

Juniper Sardonyx Furlong

Algum Almug Cubit

Hin Mite

Carbuncle Hemlock

Chestnut Ephah

Cockle

Bramble

Chrysoprasus Flax

Beryl Gerah

Money

Plants

Trees

_____

_____

_____

_____

_____

_____

_____

_____

_____

_____

_____

_____

Precious Stones

Measurements

_____

_____

_____

_____

_____

_____

_____

_____

Fill in the Blank - 2 Thessalonians Chapter 2

Use the definitions in parentheses to select the words that belong in the text and write them in the blanks. Check your answers in your Bible.

³ Let no man deceive you by any means: for that day shall not come, except there come a falling away first, and that man of sin be revealed, the son of (utter destruction) _____; ⁴ Who (acts against) _____ and (raises high) _____ himself above all that is called God, or that is worshipped; so that he as God sitteth in the temple of God, shewing himself that he is God. ⁵ Remember ye not, that, when I was yet with you, I told you these things? ⁶ And now ye know what (holds back) _____ that he might be revealed in his time. ⁷ For the (something not revealed to mankind) _____ of (wickedness) _____ doth already work: only he who now letteth will (hinder) _____, until he be taken out of the way. ⁸ And then shall that Wicked be revealed, whom the Lord shall (destroy) _____ with the spirit of his mouth, and shall destroy with the brightness of his coming: ⁹ Even him, whose coming is after the working of Satan with all power and signs and lying wonders, ¹⁰ And with all (deception) _____ of unrighteousness in them that (are eternally lost) _____; because they received not the love of the truth, that they might be saved. ¹¹ And for this cause God shall send them strong (misleading of the mind) _____, that they should believe a lie: ¹² That they all might be (condemned) _____ who believed not the truth, but had pleasure in unrighteousness. ¹³ But we are bound to give thanks alway to God for you, brethren (greatly loved) _____ of the Lord, because God hath from the beginning chosen you to salvation through (making holy) _____ of the Spirit and belief of the truth: ¹⁴ Whereunto he called you by our gospel, to the obtaining of the glory of our Lord Jesus Christ. ¹⁵ Therefore, brethren, stand (firm) _____, and hold the traditions which ye have been taught, whether by word, or our (written letter) _____.

BELOVED	EXALTETH	PERDITION
CONSUME	FAST	PERISH
DAMNED	INIQUITY	SANCTIFICATION
DECEIVABLENESS	LET	WITHHOLDETH
DELUSION	MYSTERY	
EPISTLE	OPPOSETH	

Snowflakes #2

Solution p. 123

Select a word from the word bank for each numbered clue and write it across the snowflake. When you have filled in all the answers, some of the letters on the edges will spell a word from the Bible. Write each letter on its corresponding number to reveal the word.

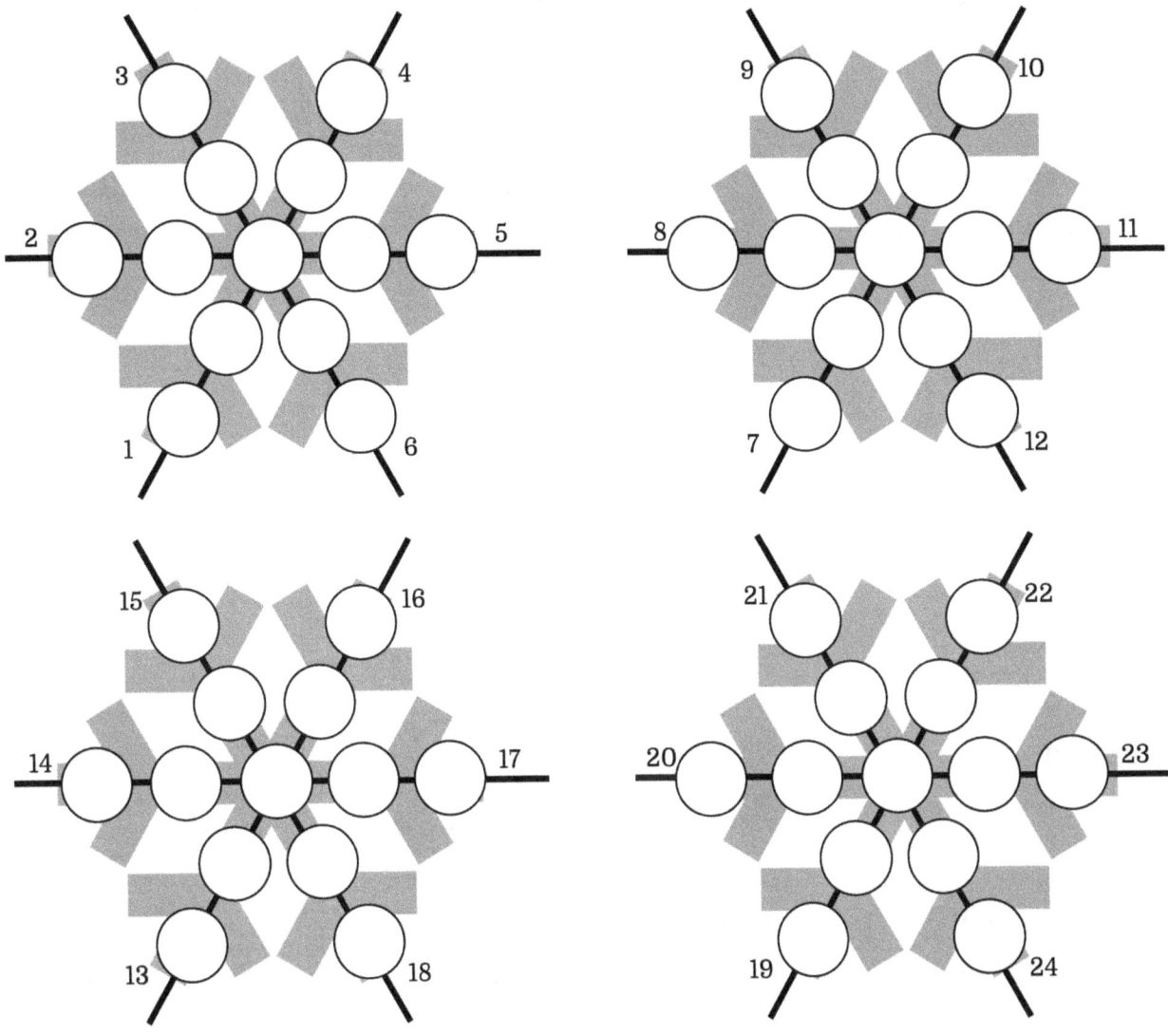

1. Headwear for a priest
2. To speak
3. A table used for sacrifice or worship
7. To change
8. To praise
9. A tenth

13. Pretend
14. Deception
15. Faulty
19. By chance
20. Venomous snake
21. Played on a wind instrument

Word Bank					
ALTAR	AMISS	FEIGN	HAPLY	PIPED	UTTER
ALTER	EXTOL	GUILE	MITRE	TITHE	VIPER

9-Letter word from Isaiah 52:13 $\_\ \_\ \ \_\ \_\ \_\ \_\ \ \_\ \_\ \_$
21 6 2 24 17 16 9 11 22

Finish the Word #3

The following verbs have the same beginning. Can you finish them, using the definitions and word lists?
The number of blanks indicates the number of missing letters.

To pardon	RE _ _ _	REBUKE
To give on demand	RE _ _ _ _	RECKON
To refresh with joy or hope	RE _ _ _ _	RECONCILE
To check or restrain	RE _ _ _ _	RECOUNT
To turn from sin	RE _ _ _ _	REGARD
To reject the authority of a ruler	RE _ _ _ _	REHEARSE
To count	RE _ _ _ _	REMIT
To go to	RE _ _ _ _	RENDER
To value or esteem	RE _ _ _ _	REPENT
To hold or keep	RE _ _ _ _	REPROACH
To tell in detail	RE _ _ _ _ _	REQUIRE
To return or replace	RE _ _ _ _ _	RESORT
To demand	RE _ _ _ _ _	RESTORE
To charge with a fault	RE _ _ _ _ _ _	RETAIN
To repeat	RE _ _ _ _ _ _	REVERENCE
To respect with fear	RE _ _ _ _ _ _ _	REVIVE
To restore friendship	RE _ _ _ _ _ _ _	REVOLT

To be necessary	BE _ _ _ _	BEFALL
To cut off the head	BE _ _ _ _	BEHEAD
To happen	BE _ _ _ _	BEHOVE
To place or store	BE _ _ _ _	BEREAVE
To pledge for a spouse	BE _ _ _ _ _	BESEECH
To ask with urgency	BE _ _ _ _ _	BESTOW
To take away from	BE _ _ _ _ _	BETHINK
To remember	BE _ _ _ _ _	BETROTH

Solution p. 120

Down the Stairs #2

Use the definitions to place words from the word bank into each row. One letter is given in each word. One word will be used twice.

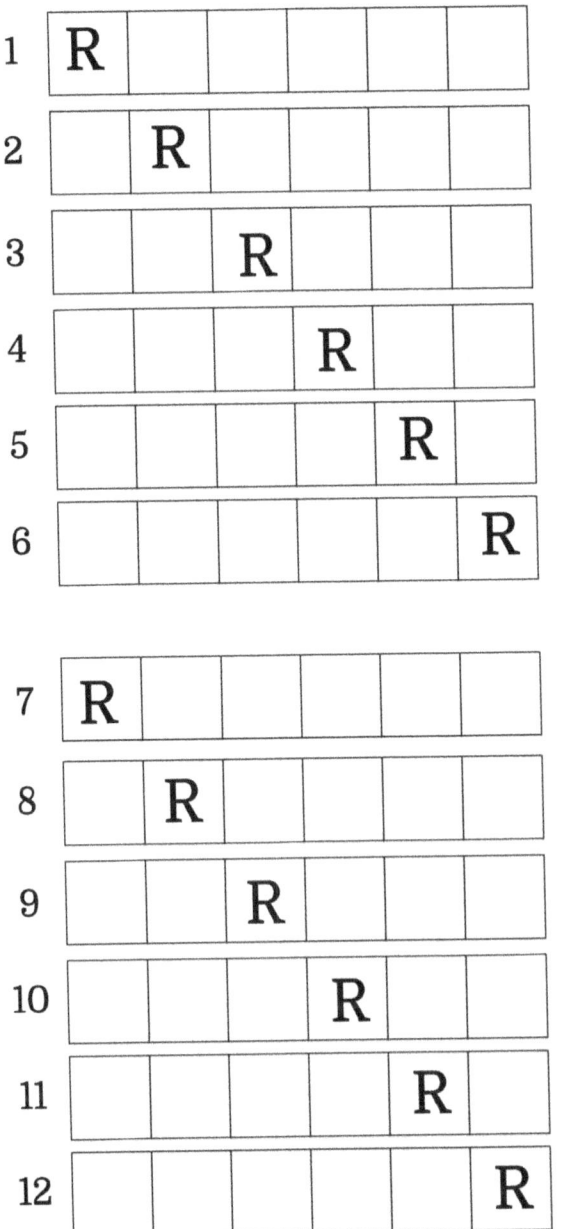

Word Bank

ALLURE
BREACH
CANKER
CHARGE
COVERT
DEARTH
EMEROD
ENDURE
GROUND
MATRIX
MURMUR
ORACLE
REBUKE
REJECT
RENOWN
REVIVE
SUNDRY
TEMPER
THRESH
THRICE
VALOUR
VERITY
WITHER

1. Chastisement
2. Foundation
3. Truth
4. Scarcity
5. To attempt to draw to
6. To lose moisture, to dry
7. To throw away
8. A revelation by God to the prophets
9. To beat
10. Tumor
11. Various
12. To mix

13. Fame
14. Break or rupture
15. Three times
16. To lay on, as a duty
17. Shelter
18. Ulcer
19. To return to life
20. The most holy place in the temple
21. Grumble
22. Womb
23. Continue
24. Bravery

Solution p. 122

41

Crossword 8

Solution p. 128

Across
2. To load
4. Early
6. Measure
10. Overcome
12. Red gemstone, garnet
13. Remain
15. To pass from one to another
16. Height of the body
17. Having knowledge
18. Small cup
21. Exhibition from God
23. Abundance

Down
1. Happen
3. Make void
5. A written letter
7. Turtle-dove
8. Attribute
9. Chastisement
11. Defensive mound
14. To despise or neglect
19. Covetousness
20. Support
22. To belong to
24. Gray

WORD BANK	ABHOR	CRUSE	LADE	STAY
	APPERTAIN	DELIVER	METE	SUPERFLUITY
	BEFALL	DISANNUL	PREVAIL	TARRY
	BETIMES	EPISTLE	RAMPART	TURTLE
	CARBUNCLE	GRISLED	REBUKE	VISITATION
	CONCUPISCENCE	IMPUTE	STATURE	WISE

Ladders

Select a word from the word bank that fits each definition. The letters inside each bolded ladder will all be the same. Solution p. 119

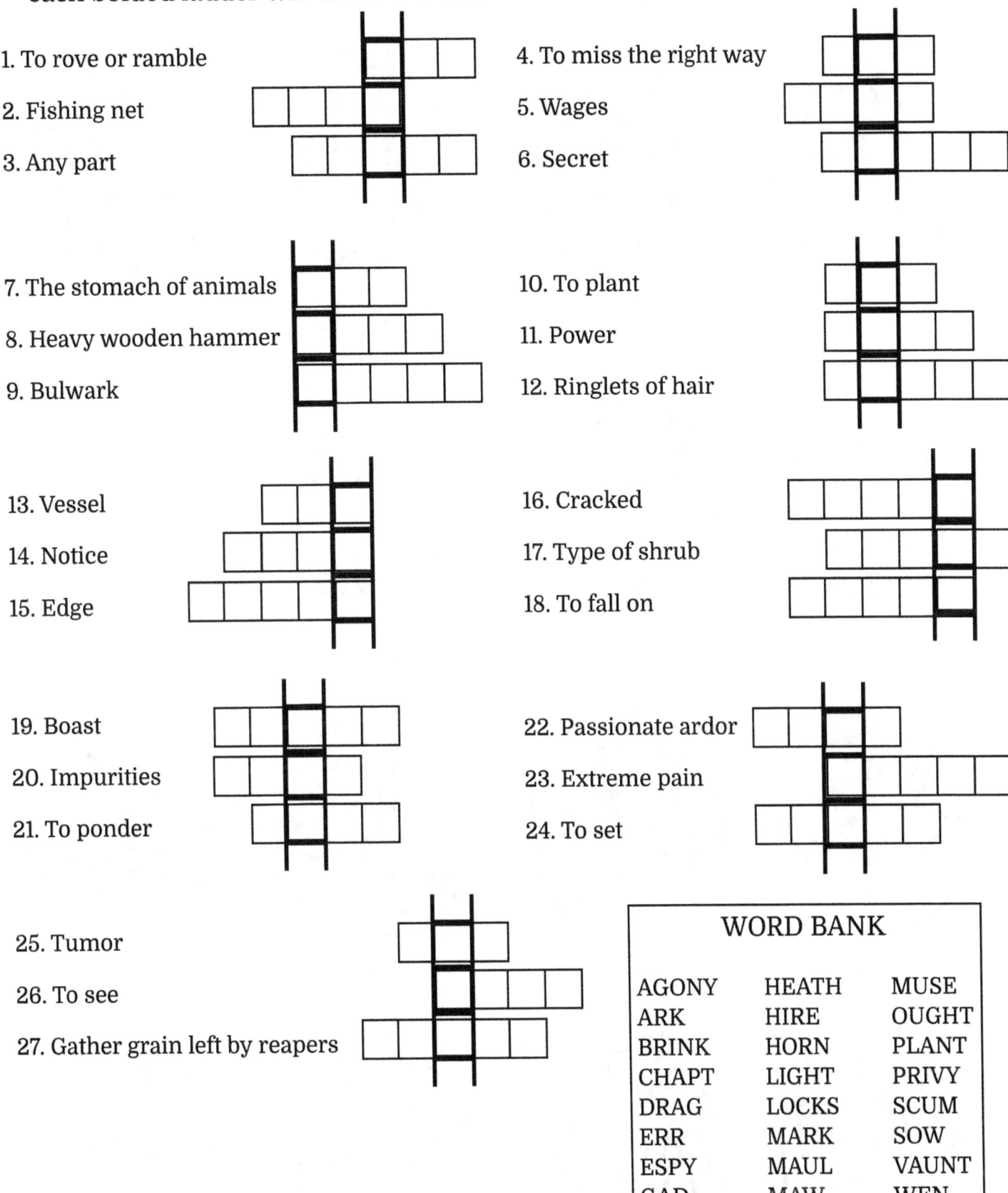

1. To rove or ramble

2. Fishing net

3. Any part

4. To miss the right way

5. Wages

6. Secret

7. The stomach of animals

8. Heavy wooden hammer

9. Bulwark

10. To plant

11. Power

12. Ringlets of hair

13. Vessel

14. Notice

15. Edge

16. Cracked

17. Type of shrub

18. To fall on

19. Boast

20. Impurities

21. To ponder

22. Passionate ardor

23. Extreme pain

24. To set

25. Tumor

26. To see

27. Gather grain left by reapers

WORD BANK

AGONY	HEATH	MUSE
ARK	HIRE	OUGHT
BRINK	HORN	PLANT
CHAPT	LIGHT	PRIVY
DRAG	LOCKS	SCUM
ERR	MARK	SOW
ESPY	MAUL	VAUNT
GAD	MAW	WEN
GLEAN	MOUNT	ZEAL

Cookie Sheet #2

Use the definitions to unscramble the letters in each cookie. Write your answers on the dotted lines.

Solution p. 124

Extreme pain — G I H S A N U

Remarkable — E O B N L A T

To polish — F H I U S R B

Seriousness — G I R T A Y V

Disagreement — N R C V A E A I

First principle — N D I E M T U R

Make attractive — U E Y B F T I A

Slyness — B Y I S U T T L

Uncivilized — A R A U R S A O B B

Unceasing — C U T O L N A I N

Weakness — T F N Y I R I M I

Puzzled — E L E D R X E P P

Abstain from — R B R E O F A

Enjoyable — A L P T A N S E

Contradict — I G N A Y S A

Watchful — I N A L I V G T

44

Synonym Scramble 2

Each set of scrambled words has a common meaning.
Use the definition as a hint. Solution p. 126

Sin

IQTYNIIU = _ _ _ _ _ _ _ _ _ _   EORSASIRNNSGT = _ _ _ _ _ _ _ _ _ _

EOFEFCN = _ _ _ _ _ _ _ _ _ _   ESTRASSP = _ _ _ _ _ _ _ _ _ _

To treat as unworthy; disdain

OMTNECN = _ _ _ _ _ _ _ _ _ _   SIPDEES = _ _ _ _ _ _ _ _ _ _

HBAOR = _ _ _ _ _ _ _ _ _ _   ERJETC = _ _ _ _ _ _ _ _ _ _

To settle or fix

ONPPTAI = _ _ _ _ _ _ _ _ _ _   AESBSHLIT = _ _ _ _ _ _ _ _ _ _

ADOIRN = _ _ _ _ _ _ _ _ _ _   ALBSHTIS = _ _ _ _ _ _ _ _ _ _

To approve or grant license

TLE = _ _ _ _ _ _ _ _ _ _   FUFESR = _ _ _ _ _ _ _ _ _ _

ALLWO = _ _ _ _ _ _ _ _ _ _   RMEIPT = _ _ _ _ _ _ _ _ _ _

To express sorrow for wrong

BMNAEO = _ _ _ _ _ _ _ _ _ _   ORUNM = _ _ _ _ _ _ _ _ _ _

ENRTEP = _ _ _ _ _ _ _ _ _ _   GTERRE = _ _ _ _ _ _ _ _ _ _

Cautious

RNEUPDT = _ _ _ _ _ _ _ _ _ _   SICEDRET = _ _ _ _ _ _ _ _ _ _

SCMITCPCREU = _ _ _ _ _ _ _ _ _ _   WERA = _ _ _ _ _ _ _ _ _ _

45

A to Z #2

Solution p. 121

The answer to each lettered clue will contain its corresponding letter **somewhere** in the word. Select carefully from the word bank!

A. One who professes to tell the future by the stars
B. The exercise of patience
C. A contract between people or states
D. To think beforehand
E. Contain
F. Adequate ability
G. House of worship for Jews
H. Celebrating victory
I. Not contrite
J. Noisy dispute
K. Humility in temper
L. Incapable of error
M. Recollection
N. The face
O. Bow or curtsy
P. Taken hold of
Q. Familiar knowledge
R. Predetermined
S. Abundance
T. Removing from one place to another
U. Severe afflictions or distresses
V. Retribution
W. Fortification
X. Explain
Y. Scriptures worn by devout Jews
Z. Object of contempt

Word Bank

ACQUAINTANCE	JANGLING
APPREHENDED	MEEKNESS
ASTROLOGER	OBEISANCE
BULWARK	PHYLACTERIES
COMPREHEND	PREMEDITATE
CONFEDERACY	REMEMBRANCE
COUNTENANCE	SUFFICIENCY
EXPOUND	SUPERFLUITY
FORBEARANCE	SYNAGOGUE
FOREORDAINED	TRANSLATION
GAZINGSTOCK	TRIBULATION
IMPENITENT	TRIUMPHING
INFALLIBLE	VENGEANCE

A _____
B _____
C _____
D _____
E _____
F _____
G _____
H _____
I _____
J _____
K _____
L _____
M _____
N _____
O _____
P _____
Q _____
R _____
S _____
T _____
U _____
V _____
W _____
X _____
Y _____
Z _____

Select-A-Syllable #3

Each of the answers to the following clues is made up of two syllables that can be found in the box. Put them together and write your completed words in the spaces provided. The numbers in parentheses indicate the total number of letters in each answer. Each syllable will be used only once.   Solution p. 121

1. Border (5) _____

2. Compare (5) _____

3. Chosen (5) _____

4. Remain (5) _____

5. Again (6) _____

6. Pan in which incense is burned (6) _____

7. Something false (6) _____

8. Active (6) _____

9. To feel pain (6) _____

10. Wrangler (7) _____

11. Great noise made by human voices (7) _____

12. Extent (7) _____

13. Perverse, disobedient (7) _____

14. Rage without reason (7) _____

15. Noxious to health, unwholesome (7) _____

16. Blight; something that hinders plant growth (8) _____

17. To form in the mind (8) _____

18. Terrible or awful (8) _____

19. A part separated from the rest (8) _____

20. Harm or hurt (8) _____

Syllable Box

A	COM	FRAG	LIM	OUR
BLAST	CON	FRESH	LIVE	PASS
BRAWL	DE	FRO	LY	RY
CEIT	DREAD	FUL	MAD	SER
CEIVE	E	ING	MENT	SOME
CEN	EN	IT	MIS	SUF
CHIEF	ER	LECT	NESS	TAR
CLAM	FER	LIK	NOI	WARD

Crossword 9

Solution p. 129

Across
3. To make alive
4. Split
8. Belonging to thee
10. Muddy
11. To follow after
14. To encircle or surround
15. Suitable
16. A great misfortune
18. Unexpectedly
21. Punish
22. Slyness
24. Prickly shrub

Down
1. Cheat
2. King's symbol of royal authority
5. Evening
6. Made an oath
7. Persistent request
9. Something taken by net
12. Dregs
13. Surrounded
17. The unlawful indulgence of lust
19. To subdue or restrain
20. Irreverent words against God
23. Merry-making

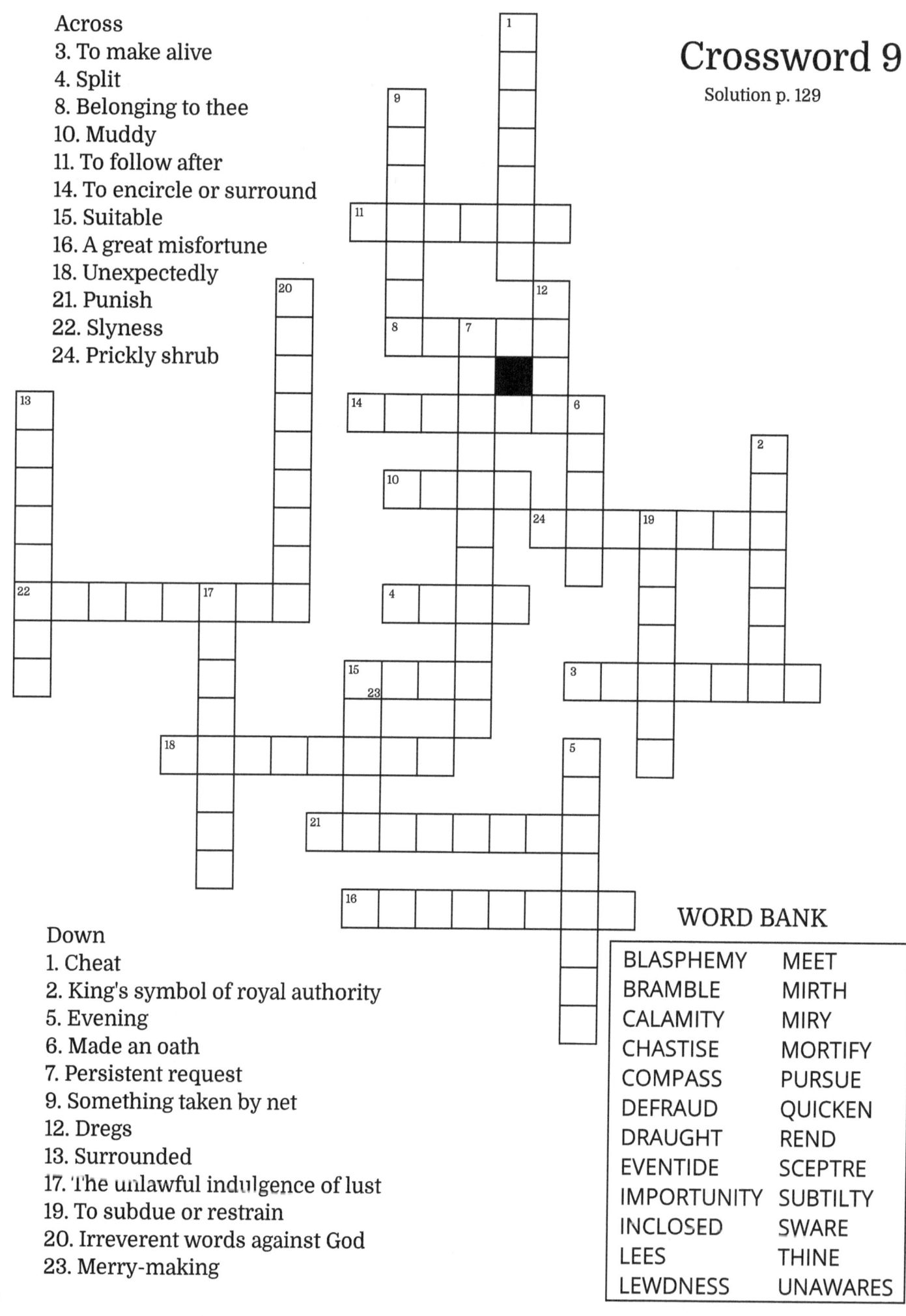

WORD BANK

BLASPHEMY	MEET
BRAMBLE	MIRTH
CALAMITY	MIRY
CHASTISE	MORTIFY
COMPASS	PURSUE
DEFRAUD	QUICKEN
DRAUGHT	REND
EVENTIDE	SCEPTRE
IMPORTUNITY	SUBTILTY
INCLOSED	SWARE
LEES	THINE
LEWDNESS	UNAWARES

Which Word?

Which of the words with similar meaning belongs in each verse? Circle your answer. Check your answers in your Bible.

Deuteronomy 25:1
If there be a _____between men, and they come unto judgment, that the judges may judge them; then they shall justify the righteous, and condemn the wicked.

          Controversy   Debate   Disputation

Psalm 44:13
Thou makest us a reproach to our neighbours, a scorn and a _____ to them that are round about us.

          Derision   Gazingstock   Hissing

Exodus 32:7
And the Lord said unto Moses, Go, get thee down; for thy people, which thou broughtest out of the land of Egypt, have _____ themselves.

          Corrupted   Defiled   Polluted

Mark 3:29
But he that shall blaspheme against the Holy Ghost hath never forgiveness, but is in danger of eternal _____.

          Condemnation   Damnation   Perdition

Proverbs 13:10
Only by pride cometh _____: but with the well advised is wisdom.

          Emulation   Contention   Strife

Proverbs 22:16
He that oppresseth the poor to increase his riches, and he that giveth to the rich, shall surely come to _____.

          Penury   Poverty   Want

Numbers 9:10
Speak unto the children of Israel, saying, If any man of you or of your _____ shall be unclean by reason of a dead body, or be in a journey afar off, yet he shall keep the passover unto the Lord.

          Lineage   Posterity   Stock

Proverbs 22:3
A _____ man foreseeth the evil, and hideth himself: but the simple pass on, and are punished.

          Circumspect   Prudent   Wise

Pinwheels #2

Solution p. 119

The answer to each numbered clue will either begin or end with the letter in the center of each pinwheel. Write a word from inside to outside or outside to inside as needed.

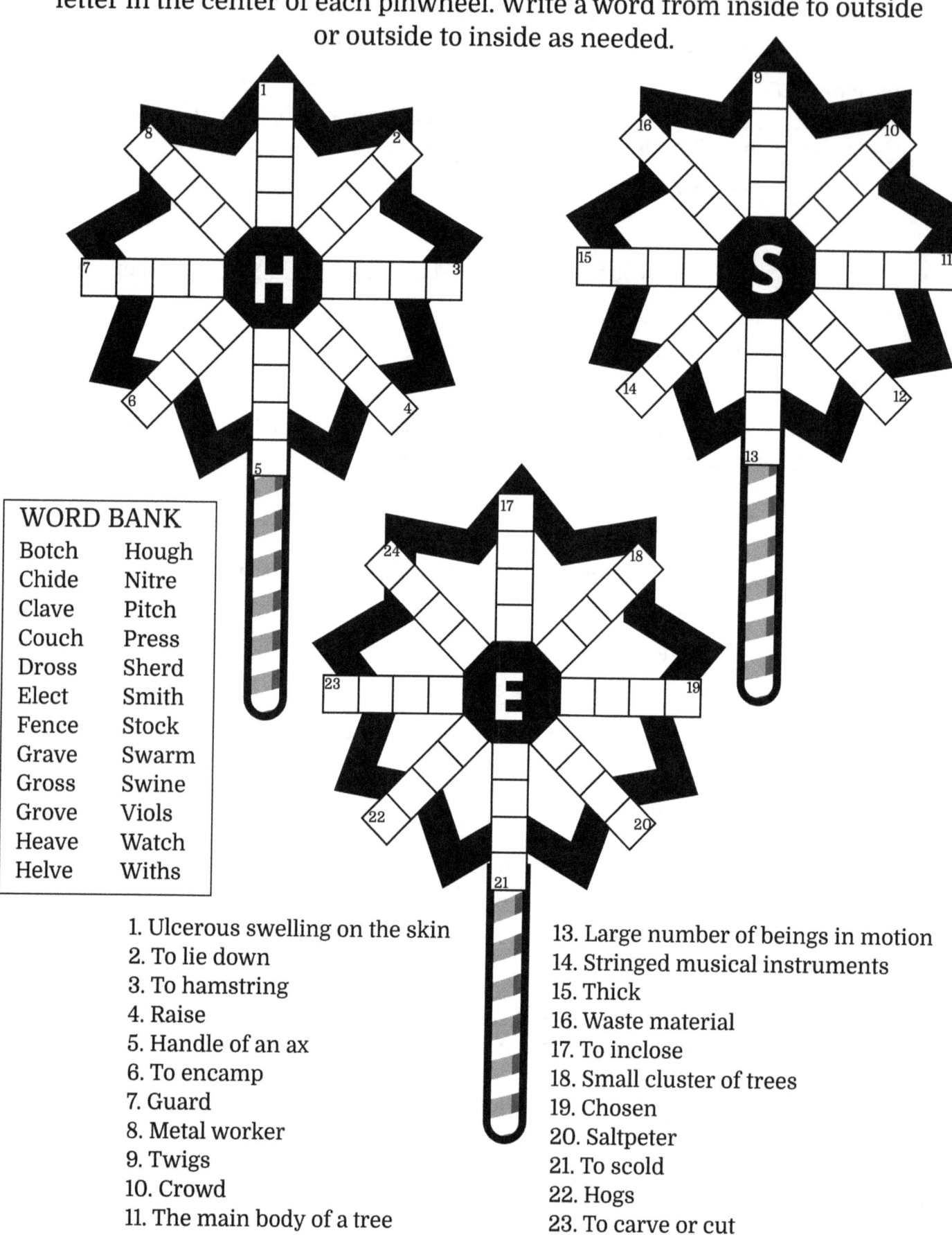

WORD BANK

Botch	Hough
Chide	Nitre
Clave	Pitch
Couch	Press
Dross	Sherd
Elect	Smith
Fence	Stock
Grave	Swarm
Gross	Swine
Grove	Viols
Heave	Watch
Helve	Withs

1. Ulcerous swelling on the skin
2. To lie down
3. To hamstring
4. Raise
5. Handle of an ax
6. To encamp
7. Guard
8. Metal worker
9. Twigs
10. Crowd
11. The main body of a tree
12. Fragment
13. Large number of beings in motion
14. Stringed musical instruments
15. Thick
16. Waste material
17. To inclose
18. Small cluster of trees
19. Chosen
20. Saltpeter
21. To scold
22. Hogs
23. To carve or cut
24. Stuck

Anagrams #3

Each word set is an anagram of a single Bible word. Use the definition to unscramble them. Stumped? Use the reference verse for help.   Solution p. 125

Example: Owing something to someone   bend diet   __indebted__

1. Meat of wild game (Genesis 27:7)   in ovens   _____
2. A new convert to a religion (Matthew 23:15)   stole prey   _____
3. Change form (Matthew 17:2)   fruit ranges   _____
4. Perseverance (Romans 2:7)   canine count   _____
5. Dangerous (2 Timothy 3:1)   pure soil   _____
6. A very hard stone (Ezekiel 3:9)   data man   _____
7. Speak evil of God (Leviticus 24:16)   lamb sheep   _____
8. Excessive (Colossians 3:5)   die on train   _____
9. Stealing (Titus 2:10)   iron plug in   _____
10. Criminals (Luke 23:32)   locate farms   _____
11. God-breathed (2 Timothy 3:16)   iron pianist   _____
12. Tight clothes (Luke 2:12)   glad winds   _____
13. That cannot decay (1 Corinthians 15:52)   burrito pencil   _____
14. Attractiveness (Isaiah 53:2)   less income   _____
15. To belong (Joshua 24:33)   earn tip   _____
16. Given to excessive eating (Luke 7:34)   lug nuts too   _____
17. Reduced to a poor state (Judges 6:6)   improves hide   _____
18. Sure (1 Kings 2:37)   cater in   _____
19. Something taken by net (Luke 5:4)   hard tug   _____
20. One who possesses great power (1 Timothy 6:15)   eat top ten   _____
21. Red gemstone (Isaiah 54:12)   clean curb   _____
22. Causing expense (2 Thessalonians 3:8)   large beach   _____
23. Violent disagreement (Acts 23:7)   sons inside   _____

Decryption

Solution p. 119

Work back and forth between the definitions and the verse above, transferring letters to the numbered spaces. Some letters will be used more than once.

___ ___ ___ ___ ___ ___ ___ ___ ___ ___ ___ ___ ___ ___ ___ ___ ___ ___ ___ ___ ___ ___ ___ ___ ___
12 44 58 30 6 31 15 11 34 26 69 32 16 20 19 21 10 7 5 37 3 27 43 46 53

___ ___ ___' ___ ___ ___ ___ ___ ___ ___ ___ ___ ___ ___ ___ ___ ___ ___ ___' ___ ___ ___
48 60 50' 56 65 47 35 17 42 70 57 24 5 62 48 59 65 23 34' 63 15 16

#1

___ ___ ___ ___ ___ ___ O B E D I E N T ___ ___ ___ ___ ___ ___ ___ ___ ___'
13 49 25 18 17 41   14 30 33 24 39 57 19 51   72 44 64 71   24 49 63 61 5'

___ ___ ___ ___ ___ ___ ___ ___ ___ ___ ___ ___ ___ ___ ___ ___ ___ ___ ___ ___ ___ ___.
33 9 6 44 38 47 49 58 33 10 51 56 67 34 61 5 49 55 2 14 46 73.

1. To preach

2. Wanderer

3. Numerous, multiplied

4. A wife of lesser status

5. One who flees

6. Exile

7. Dried

8. Filled to the full

9. Containing many inhabitants

			P				
1	2	3	4	5	6	7	8

V ___ ___ ___ ___ ___ ___ ___
9 10 11 12 13 14 15 16

___ ___ ___ ___ F ___ ___ ___
17 18 19 20 21 22 23 24

___ ___ ___ C ___ ___ ___ ___ ___
25 26 27 28 29 30 31 32 33

___ ___ G ___ ___ ___ ___ ___
34 35 36 37 38 39 40 41

___ ___ ___ ___ ___ ___ M ___ ___ ___
42 43 44 45 46 47 48 49 50 51

___ ___ ___ ___ H ___ ___
52 53 54 55 56 57 58

A ___ ___ ___ ___ ___ ___
59 60 61 62 63 64 65

___ ___ ___ U ___ ___ ___ ___
66 67 68 69 70 71 72 73

___ ___ ___ ___ ___ ___ ___ ___ ___ ___ ___ ___ ___ ___ ___ ___ ___ ___ ___ ___ ___ ___ ___ ___ ___
31 32 60 48 69 65 25 19 10 66 78 20 58 3 55 11 45 20 38 7 1 67 70 15 33

___ ___ ___ ___ ___ ___ ___ ___ ___ ___ ___ ___ ___ ___ ___ ___ ___ ___ ___ ___ ___ ___ ___ ___ ___'
24 65 6 40 26 27 13 22 59 50 46 42 30 14 73 17 58 34 28 43 76 41 8 3 63'

#2

___ ___ ___ ___ ___ ___ ___ ___ ___ ___' A C C O R D I N G ___ ___ ___ ___ ___
5 23 7 59 44 57 19 32 74 61'   12 53 56 20 21 7 17 68 18   69 3 27 32 67

___ ___ ___ ___ ___ ___ ___ ___ ___ ___ ___ ___ ___ ___ ___ ___ ___ ___ ___ ___ ___ ___ ___
42 54 49 72 2 20 75 20 55 54 42 3 43 49 68 7 48 32 52 51 14 16 43

___ ___ ___ ___ ___ ___ ___ ___ ___ ___ ___.
1 28 33 55 26 47 65 73 57 64 48.

1. Danger or peril

2. Lover

3. Lack of knowledge

4. Undercover

5. Small silver coin

6. Delightful

7. Put to death by means of a cross

8. Surprise attack

9. Offering to God

							Y
1	2	3	4	5	6	7	8

___ ___ ___ ___ M ___ ___ ___
9 10 11 12 13 14 15 16

___ ___ ___ ___ ___ ___ ___ C ___
17 18 19 20 21 22 23 24 25

S ___ ___ ___ ___ ___ ___
26 27 28 29 30 31 32

___ ___ ___ V ___ ___ ___ ___ ___ ___
33 34 35 36 37 38 39 40 41 42

___ ___ ___ ___ ___ ___ ___ ___ L ___
43 44 45 46 47 48 49 50 51 52

___ ___ ___ ___ ___ F ___
53 54 55 56 57 58 59

___ ___ B ___ ___ ___ ___ ___ ___ ___
60 61 62 63 64 65 66 67 68 69

A ___ ___ ___ ___ ___ ___ ___ ___
70 71 72 73 74 75 76 77 78

Fill in the Blank – 2 Peter Chapter 2

Use the definitions in parentheses to select the words that belong in the text and write them in the blanks. Check your answers in your Bible.

2 But there were false prophets also among the people, even as there shall be false teachers among you, who (secretly) _____ shall bring in damnable (doctrines contrary to Scripture) _____, even denying the Lord that bought them, and bring upon themselves (speedy) _____ destruction. 2 And many shall follow their (destructive) _____ ways; by reason of whom the way of truth shall be evil spoken of. 3 And through (desire to have, in a bad sense) _____ shall they with (invented) _____ words make merchandise of you: whose judgment now of a long time (delays) _____ not, and their damnation (sleeps) _____ not. 4 For if God spared not the angels that sinned, but cast them down to hell, and (committed) _____ them into chains of darkness, to be reserved unto judgment; 5 And spared not the old world, but saved Noah the eighth person, a preacher of righteousness, bringing in the flood upon the world of the ungodly; 6 And turning the cities of Sodom and Gomorrha into ashes (sentenced) _____ them with an overthrow, making them an (example) _____ unto those that after should live ungodly; 7 And delivered (righteous) _____ Lot, (troubled) _____ with the filthy (general behavior) _____ of the wicked: 8 (For that righteous man dwelling among them, in seeing and hearing, vexed his righteous soul from day to day with their unlawful deeds;) 9 The Lord knoweth how to (rescue) _____ the godly out of temptations, and to reserve the unjust unto the day of judgment to be punished: 10 But chiefly them that walk after the flesh in the lust of uncleanness, and despise government. (Overconfident) _____ are they, selfwilled, they are not afraid to speak evil of (officers of high degree) _____. 11 Whereas angels, which are greater in power and might, bring not (insulting) _____ accusation against them before the Lord.

CONDEMNED
CONVERSATION
COVETOUSNESS
DELIVER
DELIVERED
DIGNITIES
ENSAMPLE

FEIGNED
HERESIES
JUST
LINGERETH
PERNICIOUS
PRESUMPTUOUS
PRIVILY

RAILING
SLUMBERETH
SWIFT
VEXED

Crossword 10

Solution p. 129

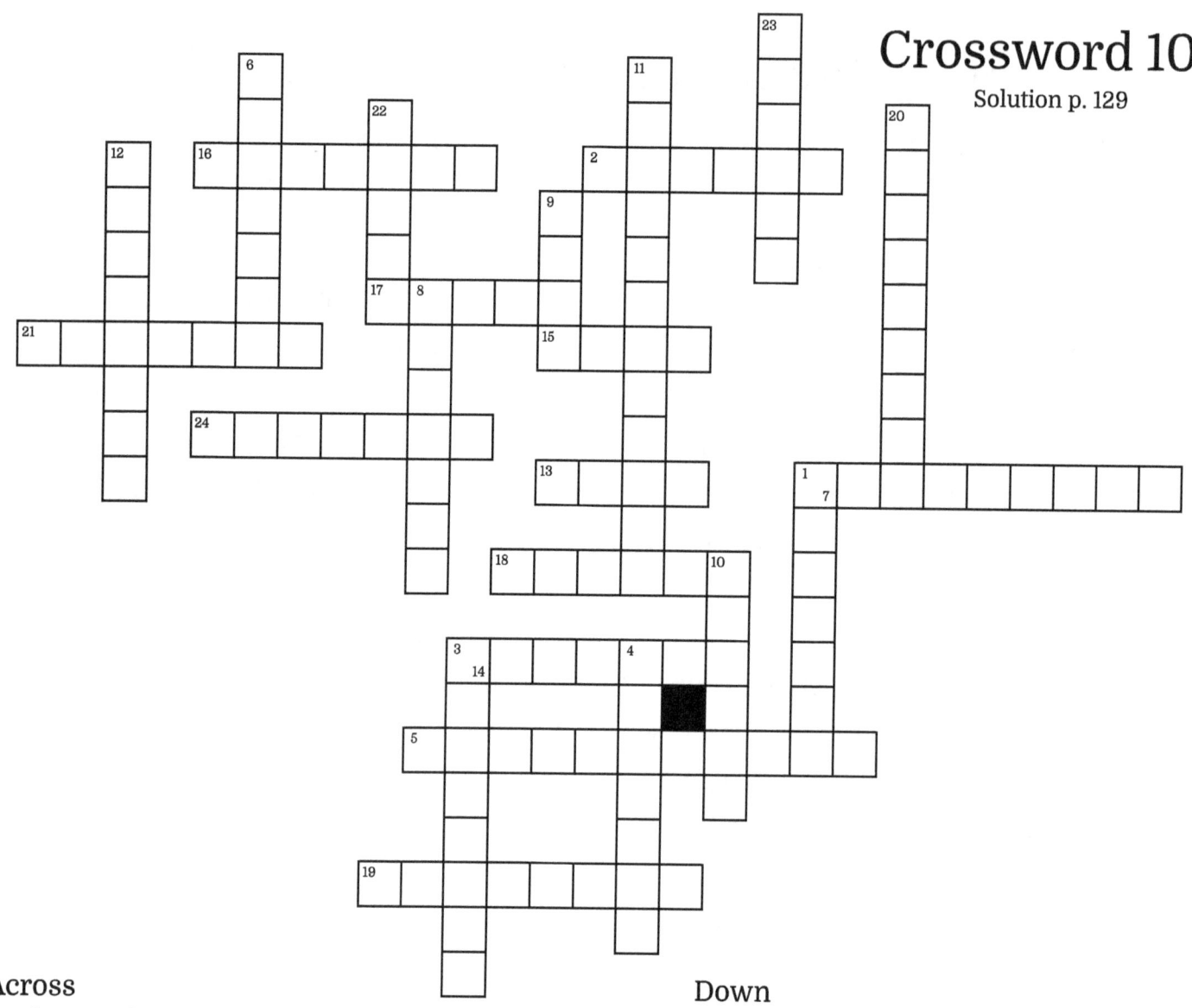

Across

2. Shame, disgrace
3. One instructed by God to announce future events
5. Greetings
7. Hallowed loaves
13. To strip the skin off an animal
15. Walked
16. Clothing
17. To eat with great eagerness
18. In two pieces
19. Trousers
21. Water bird
24. A horse drawn vehicle

Down

1. Struck and/or killed
4. Give heed
6. Large serving dish
8. Fix or establish
9. Deficiency, poverty
10. Hold or keep
11. From this time forward
12. Blight that hinders growth of plants
14. A musical instrument
20. Bow or curtsy
22. To delay or put off
23. Proper, appropriate

WORD BANK				
	APPOINT	DEFER	PROPHET	SEEMLY
	BITTERN	FLAY	PSALTERY	SHEWBREAD
	BLASTING	HEARKEN	RAIMENT	SMITTEN
	BREECHES	HENCEFORWARD	RAVIN	SUNDER
	CHARGER	INFAMY	RETAIN	TROD
	CHARIOT	OBEISANCE	SALUTATIONS	WANT

Down the Stairs #3

Use the definitions to place words from the word bank into each row. One letter is given in each word.

Solution p. 122

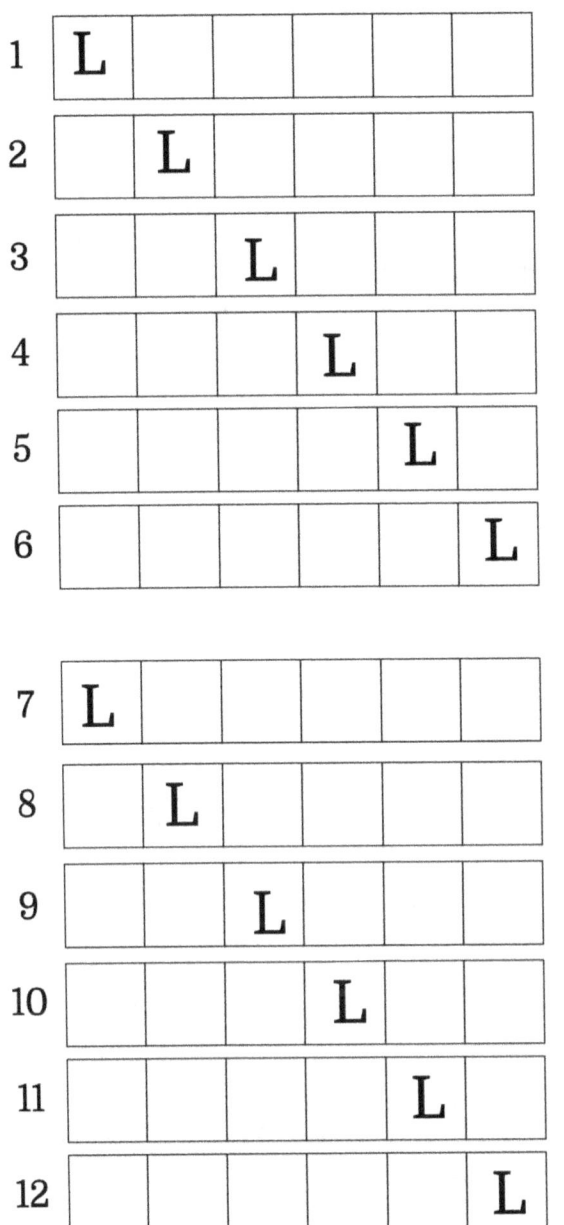

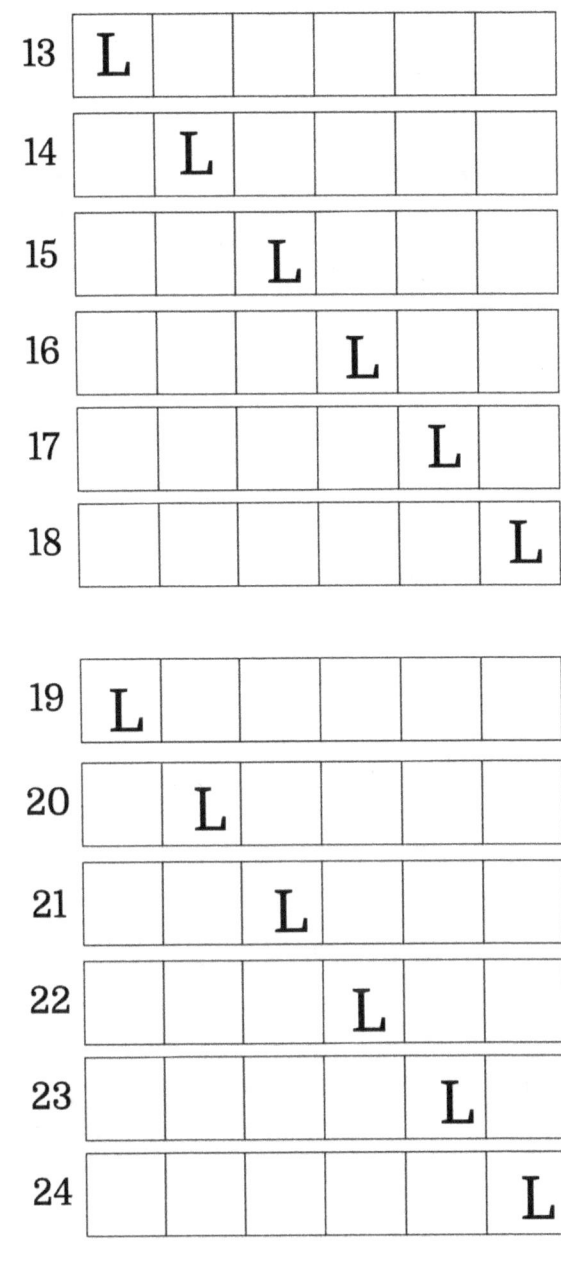

Word Bank

ALBEIT
CARNAL
CLEAVE
CLOVEN
COLOUR
FALLOW
FILLET
FOWLER
GOODLY
HALLOW
HARLOT
HOLPEN
KINDLE
LAMENT
LATTER
LEAVEN
LINTEL
MINGLE
MUTUAL
PLAGUE
SHEKEL
SIMPLE
SOLEMN
SUBTIL

1. Happening after something else
2. Notwithstanding
3. To make holy
4. Sportsman who takes wild birds
5. Unwise
6. Hebrew money
7. Part of a door frame
8. To stick to
9. Helped
10. Unplowed
11. To set on fire
12. Fleshly

13. An agent that causes dough to rise
14. Calamity or disease
15. Appearance
16. A prostitute
17. To mix
18. Sly, cunning
19. To mourn
20. Divided
21. Serious, grave
22. A little ornamental band
23. Pleasant, desirable
24. Reciprocal

Secret Word #3

Solution p. 124

Place a word from the box below on each line. The circled letters in each puzzle will spell out a secret word also found in the box (and in the Bible).

To frighten

A bud or knob

Small particle or spot

Wait

Secret Word: _____

Small piece of money

To load

To perform one's duties

To strike violently

Secret Word: _____

A solemn affirmation

Poverty or deficiency

Increase or profit

Deep mud

Secret Word: _____

Knew

Strip skin off an animal

A covering

To stop

Secret Word: _____

To measure

Gladly

Plant used for linen

A register of persons

Secret Word: _____

Accustomed

Food of any kind

The smallest part

To discern

Secret Word: _____

DASH	HAIR	METE	POLL	VAIL
FAIN	HALT	MIRE	QUIT	WAIT
FLAX	KNOP	MITE	ROOT	WANT
FLAY	LADE	MOTE	STAY	WHIT
FRAY	MAID	NAIL	TELL	WIST
GAIN	MEAT	OATH	TILL	WONT

56

Snowflakes #3

Solution p. 123

Select a word from the word bank for each numbered clue and write it across the snowflake. When you have filled in all the answers, some of the letters on the edges will spell a word from the Bible. Write each letter on its corresponding number to reveal the word.

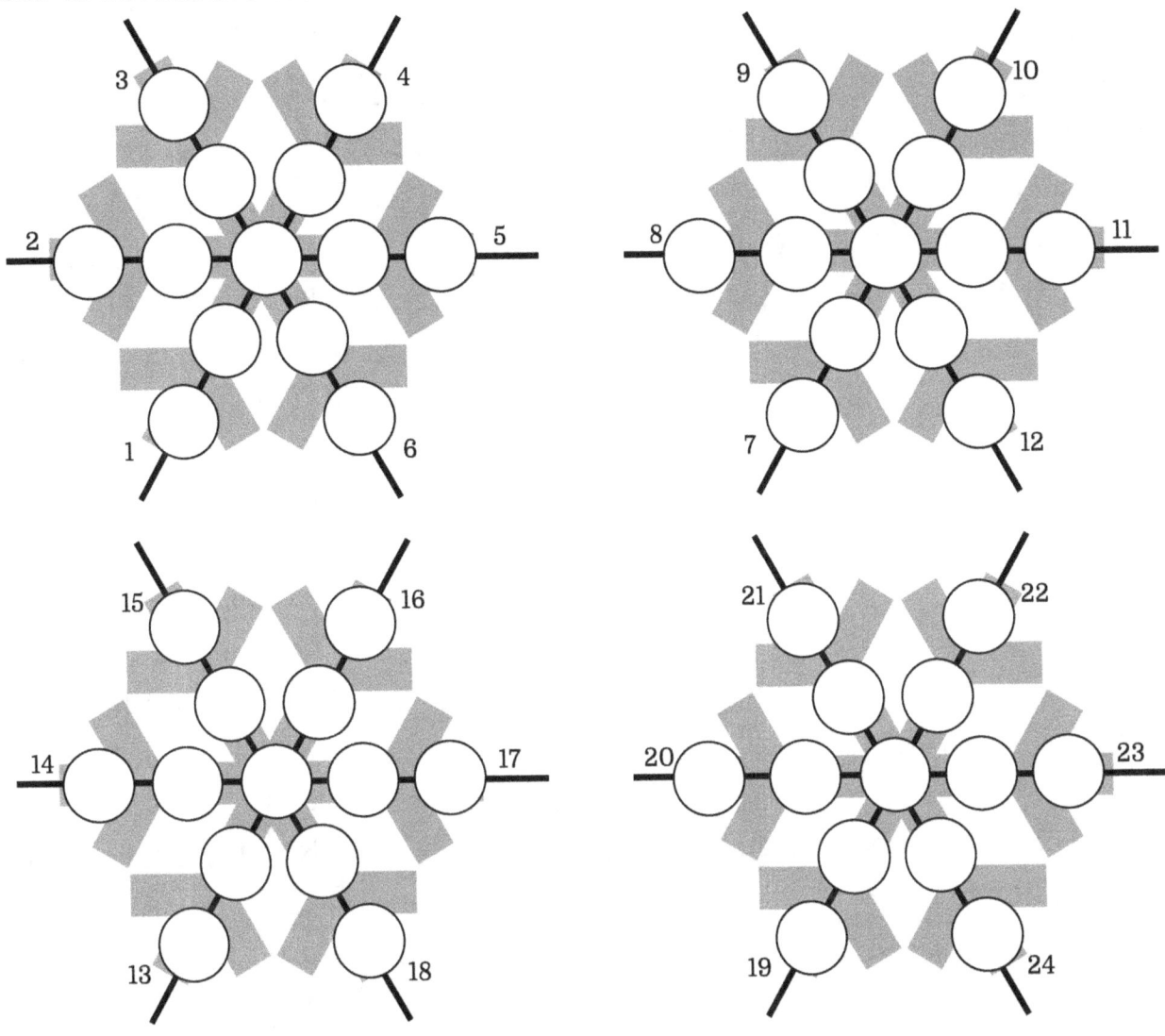

1. To invent or fabricate
2. Advantage
3. To grind the teeth
7. An idol
8. Royal jurisdiction
9. Scab

13. To attempt to find by feeling
14. Twenty
15. Pile of sheaves
19. To try
20. Able-bodied
21. To attend to in either mercy or punishment

Word Bank

ASSAY	FRAME	GROPE	LUSTY	SCALL	SHOCK
AVAIL	GNASH	IMAGE	REALM	SCORE	VISIT

8-Letter word from Matthew 9:35 _ _ _ _ _ _ _ _
21 7 5 12 19 13 4 15

Finish the Word #4

All of these nouns have the same ending. Can you finish them, using the definitions and word list? The number of blanks indicates the number of missing letters.

Definition		Word List
Fortification	_ _ _ _ TION	ABOMINATION
Distress	_ _ _ _ TION	ADMINISTRATION
A formal request	_ _ _ _ TION	AFFLICTION
A thing offered in worship	_ _ _ _ TION	COGITATION
Opposition to local civil authority	_ _ _ _ TION	CONSOLATION
Demanding with authority	_ _ _ _ TION	CONVERSATION
Calling	_ _ _ _ TION	CORRUPTION
Foretelling	_ _ _ _ _ _ TION	DESOLATION
Exhibition by God	_ _ _ _ _ _ TION	DISSIMULATION
Thinking	_ _ _ _ _ _ TION	DISTRIBUTION
Continued pain of body or mind	_ _ _ _ _ _ TION	DIVINATION
Waste or ruin	_ _ _ _ _ _ TION	EDIFICATION
Place of residence	_ _ _ _ _ _ TION	EXACTION
Decay	_ _ _ _ _ _ TION	FORNICATION
Expression of sorrow	_ _ _ _ _ _ _ TION	HABITATION
Comfort	_ _ _ _ _ _ _ TION	INQUISITION
Sexual sin by unmarried persons	_ _ _ _ _ _ _ TION	INTERPRETATION
Object of extreme hatred	_ _ _ _ _ _ _ TION	LAMENTATION
Spiritual improvement	_ _ _ _ _ _ _ TION	MUNITION
Investigation	_ _ _ _ _ _ _ TION	OBLATION
Charitable giving	_ _ _ _ _ _ _ _ TION	PETITION
Earnest request	_ _ _ _ _ _ _ _ TION	PROCLAMATION
Official notice	_ _ _ _ _ _ _ _ TION	RECONCILIATION
General behavior	_ _ _ _ _ _ _ _ TION	SEDITION
False appearance	_ _ _ _ _ _ _ _ _ TION	SIGNIFICATION
Meaning	_ _ _ _ _ _ _ _ _ TION	SUPERSCRIPTION
Engraving of letters	_ _ _ _ _ _ _ _ _ TION	SUPPLICATION
Restoration of friendship	_ _ _ _ _ _ _ _ _ TION	VEXATION
Explanation	_ _ _ _ _ _ _ _ _ TION	VISITATION
Dispensation	_ _ _ _ _ _ _ _ _ _ TION	VOCATION

Solution p. 120

Cookie Sheet #3

Use the definitions to unscramble the letters in each cookie. Write your answers on the dotted lines.

Solution p. 124

Dressed

Scattered

Opinion

Different

Wishing for

Hurtful

To coat

Perverse

Care

Merrymaking

Goods

To go with

Harsh

Agreed

Glowing hot

Abominable

59

Anagrams #4

Each word set is an anagram of a single Bible word. Use the definition to unscramble them. Stumped? Use the reference verse for help.   Solution p. 125

Example: Owing something to someone   bend diet   ___indebted_

1. Alarmed with fear (Isaiah 21:4)   fifth grade   _____
2. Of great price, very valuable (Genesis 24:53)   rice soup   _____
3. A fable or allegory (Luke 8:10)   bare lap   _____
4. Widespread disease (Jeremiah 21:6)   pet license   _____
5. Violent, intense (Jonah 4:8)   even them   _____
6. What is left after a part is taken (Isaiah 38:10)   dire use   _____
7. Abundant (Psalm 86:15)   pulse tone   _____
8. Favoring success (Zechariah 8:12)   poor purses   _____
9. To afflict or harass (Psalm 109:16)   pet rescue   _____
10. One who betrays trust (Luke 6:16)   rat trio   _____
11. A type of soup (Genesis 25:34)   pet goat   _____
12. Falsehood, lies (Psalm 5:6)   gas line   _____
13. Pretender (Matthew 6:2)   ice trophy   _____
14. Estranged (Ezekiel 23:22)   a lean diet   _____
15. That which is inherited (Exodus 6:8)   their age   _____
16. Something that furnishes proof (Hebrews 11:4)   wins set   _____
17. Quarrelsome (Proverbs 26:21)   cute notions   _____
18. Excessive feeding (Luke 21:34)   tiger is fun   _____
19. Mediation (Romans 8:34)   is not sincere _____
20. Not to be appeased (Romans 1:31)   llama bicep   _____
21. Disapproved (Numbers 30:8)   dad lies low   _____
22. Public civil officer (Ezra 7:25)   aim targets   _____

Crossword 11

Solution p. 129

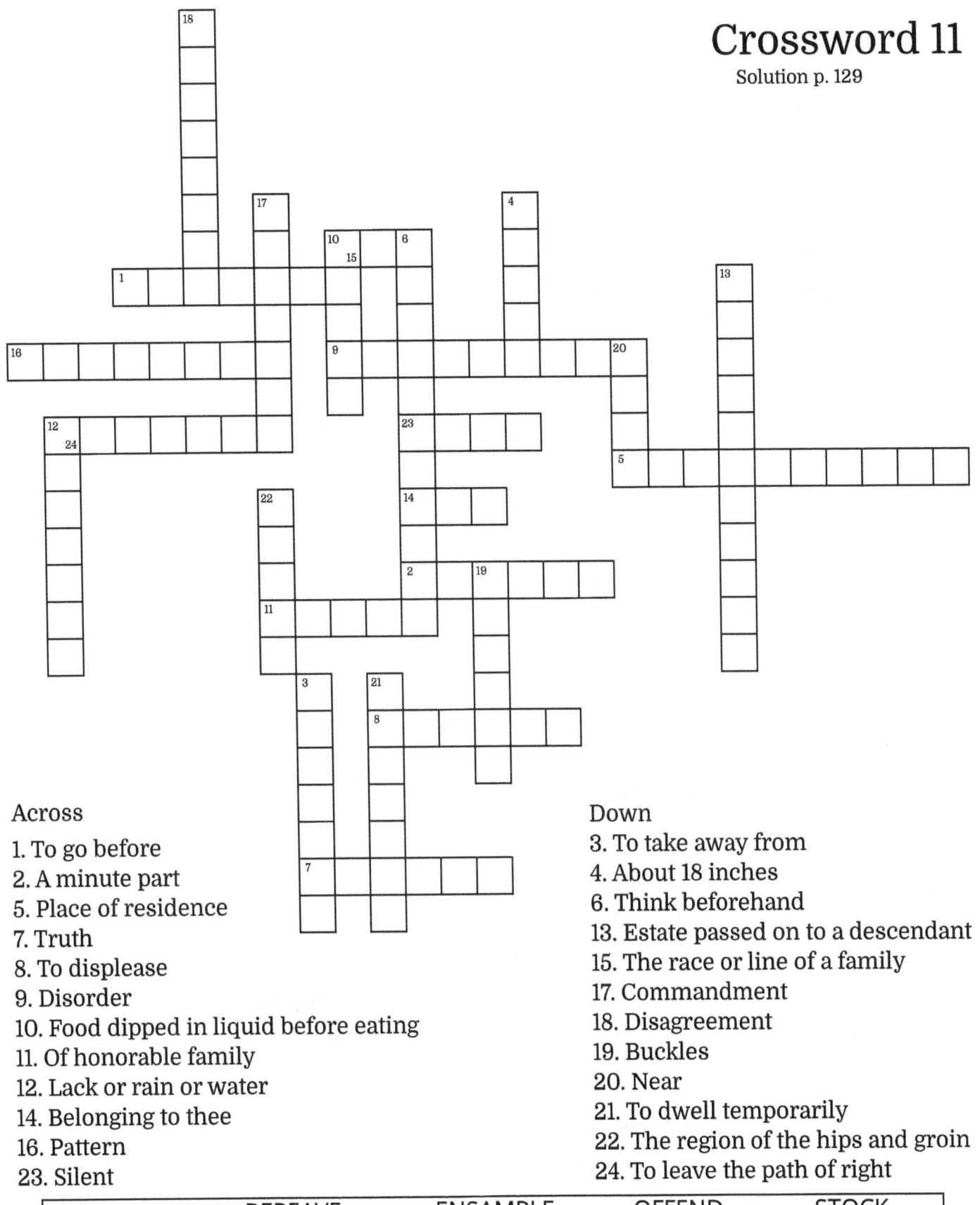

Across

1. To go before
2. A minute part
5. Place of residence
7. Truth
8. To displease
9. Disorder
10. Food dipped in liquid before eating
11. Of honorable family
12. Lack or rain or water
14. Belonging to thee
16. Pattern
23. Silent

Down

3. To take away from
4. About 18 inches
6. Think beforehand
13. Estate passed on to a descendant
15. The race or line of a family
17. Commandment
18. Disagreement
19. Buckles
20. Near
21. To dwell temporarily
22. The region of the hips and groin
24. To leave the path of right

WORD BANK			
BEREAVE	ENSAMPLE	OFFEND	STOCK
COMMOTION	HABITATION	PRECEPT	TACHES
CUBIT	INHERITANCE	PREMEDITATE	THY
DECLINE	LOINS	PREVENT	TITTLE
DROUGHT	NIGH	SOJOURN	VARIANCE
DUMB	NOBLE	SOP	VERITY

61

Picture Match #2

Each of the following verses contains a reference to an item pictured. Use the letters on the pictures to match them to the correct verse.   Solution p. 125

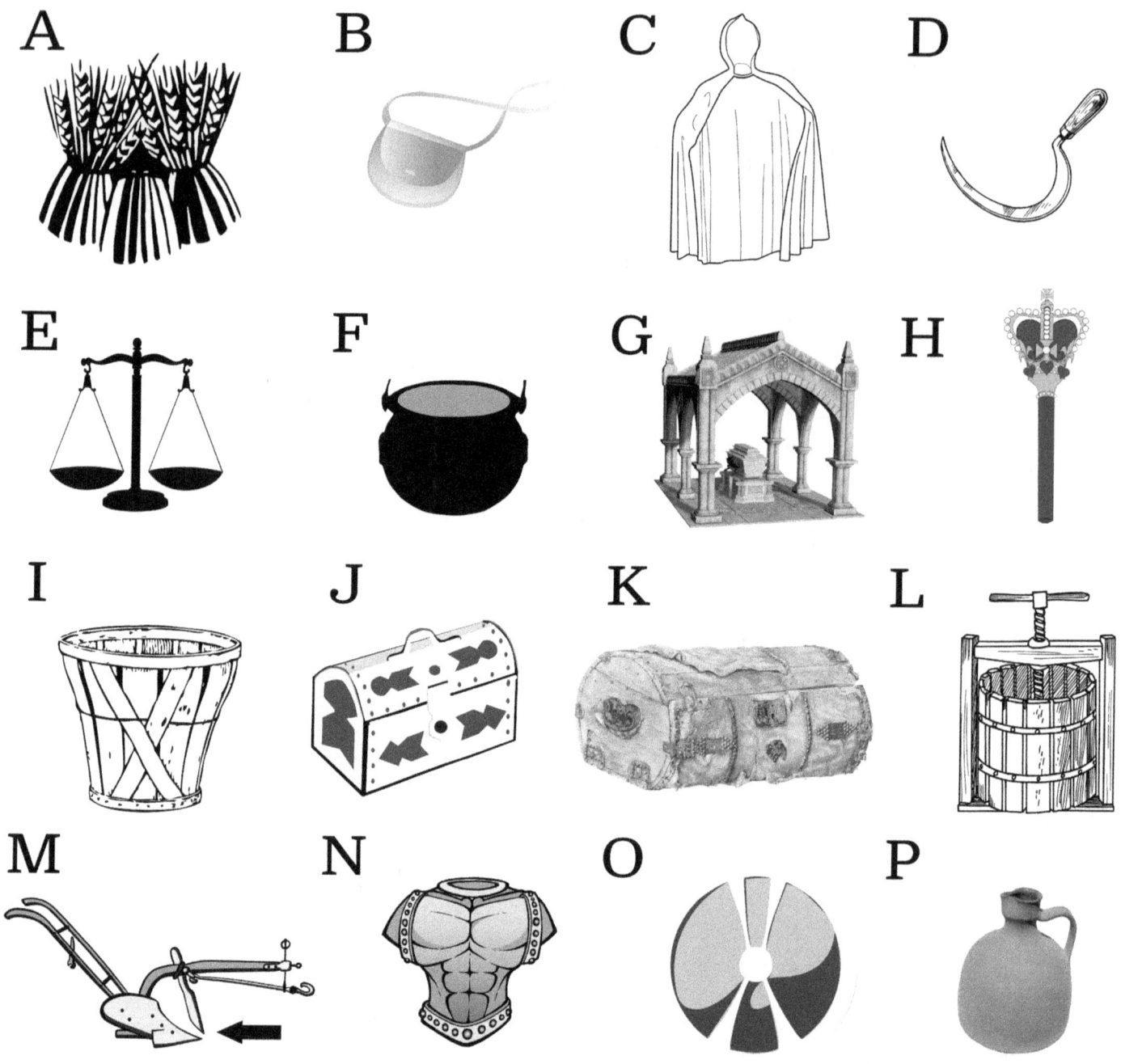

1. _ _ _ _ _   1 Kings 17:14
   For thus saith the Lord God of Israel, The barrel of meal shall not waste, neither shall the cruse of oil fail, until the day that the Lord sendeth rain upon the earth.

2. _ _ _ _ _   Mark 12:41
   And Jesus sat over against the treasury, and beheld how the people cast money into the treasury: and many that were rich cast in much.

3. _ _ _ _ _   Exodus 39:23
   And there was an hole in the midst of the robe, as the hole of an habergeon, with a band round about the hole, that it should not rend.

4. _____ Revelation 14:16
And he that sat on the cloud thrust in his sickle on the earth; and the earth was reaped.

5. _____ 2 Chronicles 35:13
And they roasted the passover with fire according to the ordinance: but the other holy offerings sod they in pots, and in caldrons, and in pans, and divided them speedily among all the people.

6. _____ Proverbs 11:1
A false balance is abomination to the Lord: but a just weight is his delight.

7. _____ Psalm 126:6
He that goeth forth and weepeth, bearing precious seed, shall doubtless come again with rejoicing, bringing his sheaves with him.

8. _____ Mark 6:8
And commanded them that they should take nothing for their journey, save a staff only; no scrip, no bread, no money in their purse:

9. _____ Isaiah 5:2
And he fenced it, and gathered out the stones thereof, and planted it with the choicest vine, and built a tower in the midst of it, and also made a winepress therein: and he looked that it should bring forth grapes, and it brought forth wild grapes.

10. _____ Job 1:20
Then Job arose, and rent his mantle, and shaved his head, and fell down upon the ground, and worshipped,

11. _____ 2 Kings 9:28
And his servants carried him in a chariot to Jerusalem, and buried him in his sepulchre with his fathers in the city of David.

12. _____ Esther 5:2
And it was so, when the king saw Esther the queen standing in the court, that she obtained favour in his sight: and the king held out to Esther the golden sceptre that was in his hand. So Esther drew near, and touched the top of the sceptre.

13. _____ Psalm 18:30
As for God, his way is perfect: the word of the Lord is tried: he is a buckler to all those that trust in him.

14. _____ Isaiah 2:4
And he shall judge among the nations, and shall rebuke many people: and they shall beat their swords into plowshares, and their spears into pruninghooks: nation shall not lift up sword against nation, neither shall they learn war any more.

15. _____ Matthew 5:15
Neither do men light a candle, and put it under a bushel, but on a candlestick; and it giveth light unto all that are in the house.

16. _____ Acts 21:15
And after those days we took up our carriages, and went up to Jerusalem.

Synonym Scramble 3

Each set of scrambled words has a common meaning.
Use the definition as a hint.

Solution p. 126

To test

PMTET = _ _ _ _ _ _ _ _ _ _ 　　　PREVO = _ _ _ _ _ _ _ _ _ _

TYR = _ _ _ _ _ _ _ _ _ _ 　　　IEANMXE = _ _ _ _ _ _ _ _ _ _

To make known

ABYREW = _ _ _ _ _ _ _ _ _ _ 　　　EWSH = _ _ _ _ _ _ _ _ _ _

ATBYRE = _ _ _ _ _ _ _ _ _ _ 　　　SCSOILED = _ _ _ _ _ _ _ _ _ _

Great anger

COELHR = _ _ _ _ _ _ _ _ _ _ 　　　UFYR = _ _ _ _ _ _ _ _ _ _

IINAIONNGTD = _ _ _ _ _ _ _ _ _ _ 　　　RTWHA = _ _ _ _ _ _ _ _ _ _

A mandate given by an authority

DOMENMCATNM = _ _ _ _ _ _ _ _ _ _ 　　　ECRPPET = _ _ _ _ _ _ _ _ _ _

TTESAUT = _ _ _ _ _ _ _ _ _ _ 　　　ONIERDCAN = _ _ _ _ _ _ _ _ _ _

Shame

MNIOYIGN = _ _ _ _ _ _ _ _ _ _ 　　　INYMAF = _ _ _ _ _ _ _ _ _ _

HRCERAOP = _ _ _ _ _ _ _ _ _ _ 　　　ACGDIRSE = _ _ _ _ _ _ _ _ _ _

Entirely

EYPCRELTF = _ _ _ _ _ _ _ _ _ _ 　　　LOHWLY = _ _ _ _ _ _ _ _ _ _

ACLEN = _ _ _ _ _ _ _ _ _ _ 　　　RLETYUT = _ _ _ _ _ _ _ _ _ _

Double Trouble #2

Solution p. 119

Place the correct set of missing double letters into each blank using the definitions as your guide. Some words will have more than one set of doubles.

1. Instrument used to level soil and break up clods   H A _ _ O W S
2. Depravity   V I _ _ A N Y
3. To move unsteadily; to reel   S T A _ _ E R
4. An aromatic plant similar to cinnamon   C A _ _ I A
5. Hoe   M A _ _ O C K
6. Instrument of execution by hanging   G A _ _ O W S
7. Excommunicated   A _ _ U R S E D
8. One who pleads for another   I N T E R C E _ _ O R
9. Of healthy skin   R U _ _ Y
10. Line of ancestors   P E D I G R _ _
11. To take the place of   S U _ _ L A N T
12. Perfections   T H U _ _ I M
13. Incident   O _ _ U _ _ E N T
14. To give to another   C O _ _ U N I C A T E
15. Bandage   R O _ _ E R
16. Showy and powerful   G A _ _ A N T
17. Trade   T R A _ _ I C K
18. Leather bag used for blowing a fire   B E _ _ O W S
19. Armor   H A R N E _ _
20. To faint   S W _ _ N
21. Work of wood or iron made of crossing bars to form open squares   L A _ _ I C E
22. Stupid   S O _ _ I S H
23. Saliva   S P I _ _ L E
24. To have as owner   P O _ _ E _ _
25. State of being overburdened   O _ _ R E _ _ I O N

LETTER BANK

CC	FF	LL	MM	RR	SS	TT
CC	GG	LL	OO	RR	SS	TT
DD	LL	LL	PP	SS	SS	TT
EE	LL	MM	PP	SS	SS	TT

Select-A-Syllable #4

Each of the answers to the following clues is made up of two syllables that can be found in the box. Put them together and write your completed words in the spaces provided. The numbers in parentheses indicate the total number of letters in each answer. Each syllable will be used only once.   Solution p. 121

1. The breast area (5)

2. Any person whatever (5)

3. Sign (5)

4. To order or direct (6)

5. One who enters into a bond for another (6)

6. Something of value paid to an authority (7)

7. To help or assist (7)

8. Impediment or stumblingblock (7)

9. Mixed (7)

10. Obedient (7)

11. Utmost degree of misery (7)

12. Large serving dish (7)

13. To overload or burden (7)

14. Anointing (7)

15. Delude or deceive (7)

16. Humble; penitent (8)

17. To increase, to be prosperous (8)

18. Someone working for wages (8)

19. To lose strength, to pine (8)

20. Risk, hazard (7)

Syllable Box

BE	FLOUR	KEN	SO	TRIB
BO	GLED	LAN	SOM	TRITE
CHARG	GUILE	LING	SUB	TURE
CON	GUISH	MENT	SUC	TY
COUR	HIRE	MIN	SURE	UNC
EN	ISH	OF	TION	UTE
ER	JECT	OP	TO	VEN
FENCE	JOIN	PRESS	TOR	WHO

Crossword 12

Solution p. 129

Across
2. Free by paying a price
3. To know
5. Two
8. Deep sorrow on account of sin
9. Interest paid on a loan
10. Excellent, splendid
11. To call to action, to incite
14. Terrible
15. Without pause
17. Buck
18. Deception
19. Thick

Down
1. Violation of law
4. A register of persons
6. Continued pain of body or mind
7. Harm, hurt
12. For which reason, why
13. To make uneasy or restless
16. To have power over
20. Insane, or someone who is
21. A measure of weight
22. One who professes to tell the future by positions of the stars
23. A lentil, bean, or pea
24. Afflict or harass

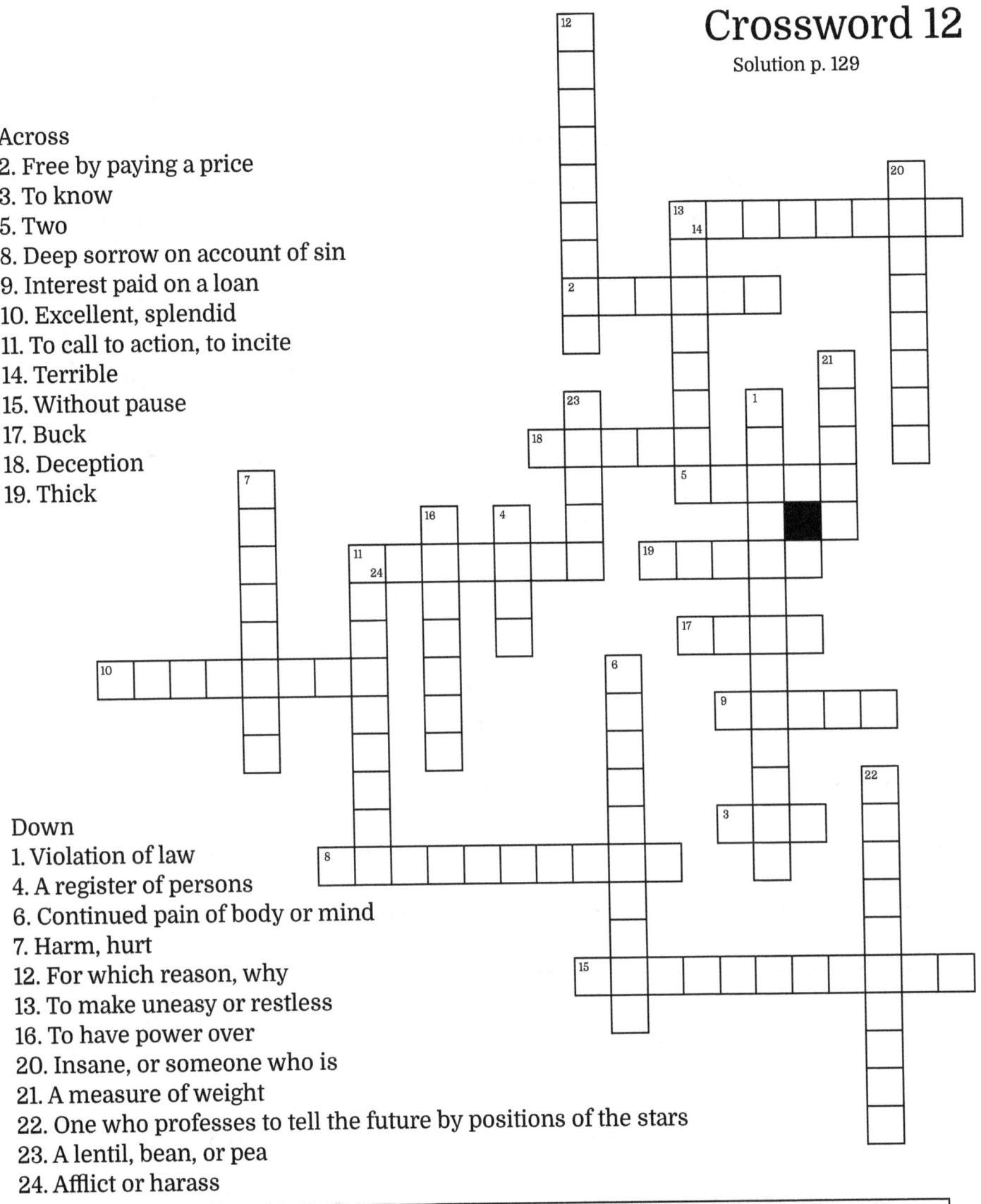

WORD BANK	AFFLICTION	GROSS	POLL	REPENTANCE
	ASTROLOGER	GUILE	POSSESS	TRANSGRESSION
	CONTINUALLY	HART	POUND	TWAIN
	DISQUIET	LUNATICK	PROVOKE	USURY
	DREADFUL	MISCHIEF	PULSE	WHEREFORE
	GLORIOUS	PERSECUTE	RANSOM	WOT

Sort Them Out #2

Write each word under the correct category. Each answer will be used only once.

Solution p. 120

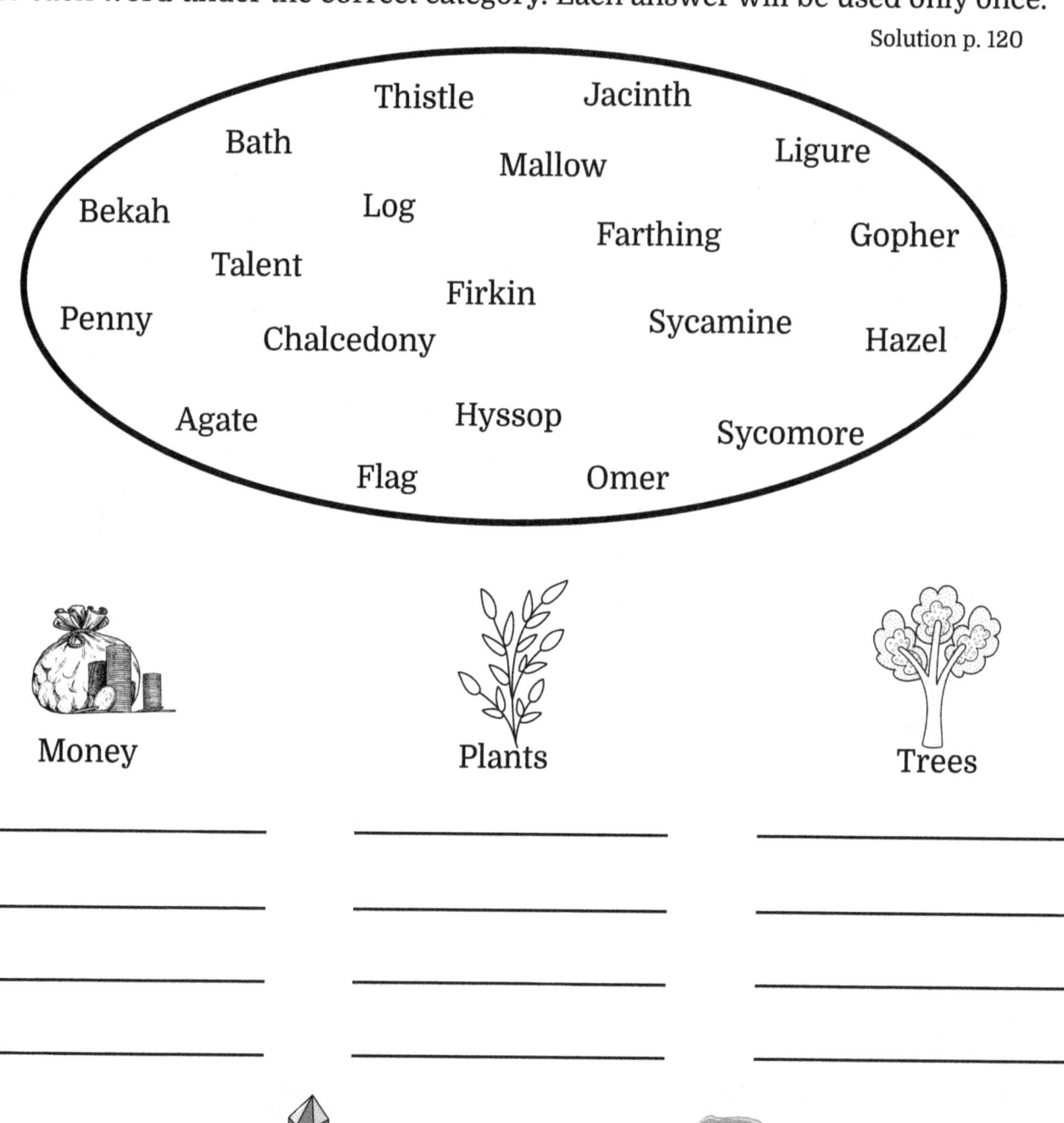

Thistle   Jacinth

Bath   Mallow   Ligure

Bekah   Log   Farthing   Gopher

Talent

Firkin

Penny   Sycamine   Hazel

Chalcedony

Agate   Hyssop   Sycomore

Flag   Omer

Money

Plants

Trees

_____   _____   _____

_____   _____   _____

_____   _____   _____

_____   _____   _____

Precious Stones

Measurements

_____   _____

_____   _____

_____   _____

_____   _____

A to Z #3

The answer to each lettered clue will contain its corresponding letter **somewhere** in the word. Select carefully from the word bank!

A. Full confidence
B. Four-faced beings depicted on the mercy seat
C. Combination of people for an evil purpose
D. Not having; needy
E. Bashfulness
F. Enough
G. Extreme limits
H. To fill
I. Idea of the mind
J. To dwell temporarily
K. To own, avow, or assent to be true
L. Looseness, lustfulness
M. Complaints
N. One who lives in a certain place
O. Payback
P. Bias of judgment
Q. To call to account for
R. Deep sorrow on account of sin
S. Begged; implored
T. Moderation
U. Without pause
V. Prosperous state
W. Bitter plant of Revelation
X. Between
Y. Quietness
Z. Fear

Word Bank

ACKNOWLEDGE	MURMURINGS
ADVANTAGE	OUTGOINGS
AMAZEMENT	PARTIALITY
ASSURANCE	RECOMPENCE
BESOUGHT	REPENTANCE
BETWIXT	REPLENISH
CHERUBIM	REQUIRE
CONSPIRACY	SHAMEFACEDNESS
CONTINUALLY	SOJOURN
DESTITUTE	SUFFICIENT
IMAGINATION	TEMPERANCE
INHABITANT	TRANQUILLITY
LASCIVIOUSNESS	WORMWOOD

A _____
B _____
C _____
D _____
E _____
F _____
G _____
H _____
I _____
J _____
K _____
L _____
M _____
N _____
O _____
P _____
Q _____
R _____
S _____
T _____
U _____
V _____
W _____
X _____
Y _____
Z _____

Common Denominator #2

Each of the answers to the following clues is made up of three segments (NOT syllables). The words have one segment in common which is in its correct position. Choose the others from the box and write them in the spaces provided.

Solution p. 132

Clue	Beginning	Middle	End
1. Stifle or put out	___	EN	___
2. Seeds used for food	___	EN	___
3. Eagerly devouring	___	EN	___
4. Worthy of worship	___	EN	___
5. Heart, liver, and lungs of an animal	___	EN	___
6. To repay, requite	___	EN	___
7. Release from distress	EN	___	___
8. One who vindicates	___	EN	___
9. Not raised by yeast	___	EN	___
10. Mournful	___	EN	___
11. Civil or military officer	___	EN	___
12. Having fallen into a worse state	___	EN	___
13. Exciting	EN	___	___
14. False appearance, feigning	___	EN	___
15. Taxes and duties collected by the state	___	EN	___

SEGMENTS

ANCE	DEG	L	PRET	REVER
ANT	ED	LAM	PURT	SE
AV	ERATE	LARGE	QU	TABLE
CE	FLAM	LIEUT	RAV	TILES
CH	GER	MENT	RECOMP	UE
D	ING	OUS	REV	UNLEAV

Finish the Word #5

The following words have the same ending. Can you finish them, using the definitions and word list? The number of blanks indicates the number of missing letters.

Clue	Answer blanks	Word List
Totally, entirely	_ _ _ _ LY	ASSUREDLY
Sacredly	_ _ _ _ LY	BITTERLY
Truly	_ _ _ _ LY	CHIEFLY
Having strategy	_ _ _ _ LY	COMFORTABLY
Totally	_ _ _ _ _ LY	CONTINUALLY
Privately or secretly	_ _ _ _ _ LY	DELICATELY
For the most part	_ _ _ _ _ LY	EARNESTLY
With speed	_ _ _ _ _ LY	EXCEEDINGLY
Proudly	_ _ _ _ _ LY	HASTILY
Harshly	_ _ _ _ _ LY	HAUGHTILY
Strictly	_ _ _ _ _ _ LY	HOLILY
In a severe manner	_ _ _ _ _ _ LY	LOFTILY
Unbecoming	_ _ _ _ _ _ LY	MORTALLY
Premature	_ _ _ _ _ _ LY	PRESENTLY
In a manner that must cause death	_ _ _ _ _ _ LY	PRIVILY
Cunningly	_ _ _ _ _ _ LY	ROUGHLY
Proudly	_ _ _ _ _ _ _ LY	SKILFULLY
Soon after	_ _ _ _ _ _ _ LY	STEDFASTLY
Honestly	_ _ _ _ _ _ _ LY	STRAITLY
Certainly	_ _ _ _ _ _ _ LY	SUBTILLY
With dexterity	_ _ _ _ _ _ _ LY	SUMPTUOUSLY
With strength and bravery	_ _ _ _ _ _ _ LY	UNSEEMLY
Eagerly	_ _ _ _ _ _ _ LY	UNTIMELY
Tenderly	_ _ _ _ _ _ _ _ LY	UNWITTINGLY
Firmly	_ _ _ _ _ _ _ _ LY	UPRIGHTLY
Without pause	_ _ _ _ _ _ _ _ _ LY	UTTERLY
In a manner that gives consolation	_ _ _ _ _ _ _ _ _ LY	VALIANTLY
To a very great degree	_ _ _ _ _ _ _ _ _ LY	VERILY
Splendidly	_ _ _ _ _ _ _ _ _ LY	WHOLLY
Without knowledge	_ _ _ _ _ _ _ _ _ LY	WILILY

Solution p. 120

Cookie Sheet #4

Use the definitions to unscramble the letters in each cookie. Write your answers on the dotted lines.

Solution p. 124

Pardon

Unbeliever

Waves

Great feast

Agreement

Uninhabited

Residence

Heroic acts

Enemy

Misfortune

Sincere

Shaking

Public toilet

False praise

Make great

Insane

M_ss_ng V_w_ls

#2

(Missing Vowels) Fill in the missing vowels to form some commonly used adverbs. You will notice that the same meaning may apply to more than one word.

Solution p. 122

In this	h _ r _ _ n
While	wh _ lst
Up until this time	h _ r _ _ nt _
In whatever place	wh _ r _ s _ _ v _ r
Nevertheless	n _ tw _ thst _ nd _ ng
With what	wh _ r _ w _ th _ l
So that	_ ns _ m _ ch
To which	wh _ r _ _ nt _
Rightly	_ r _ ght
To this place	h _ th _ r
In that or this place, time, or thing	th _ r _ _ n
Be it so	_ lb _ _ t
To whatever place	wh _ th _ rs _ _ v _ r
In spite of that	n _ v _ rth _ l _ ss
Seeing that	f _ rs _ m _ ch
To that or this	th _ r _ _ nt _
Often	_ ft
Prior in time	_ f _ r _
Immediately	str _ _ ghtw _ _
To that degree	_ ns _ m _ ch
Immediately	_ n _ n
On that or this	th _ r _ _ n
Seeing that	f _ r _ sm _ ch
At all; in any fashion	s _ _ v _ r
From that place	th _ nc _
Unexpectedly	_ n _ w _ r _ s
Formerly	h _ r _ t _ f _ r _
Immediately	f _ rthw _ th
Early	b _ t _ m _ s

73

Crossword 13

Solution p. 130

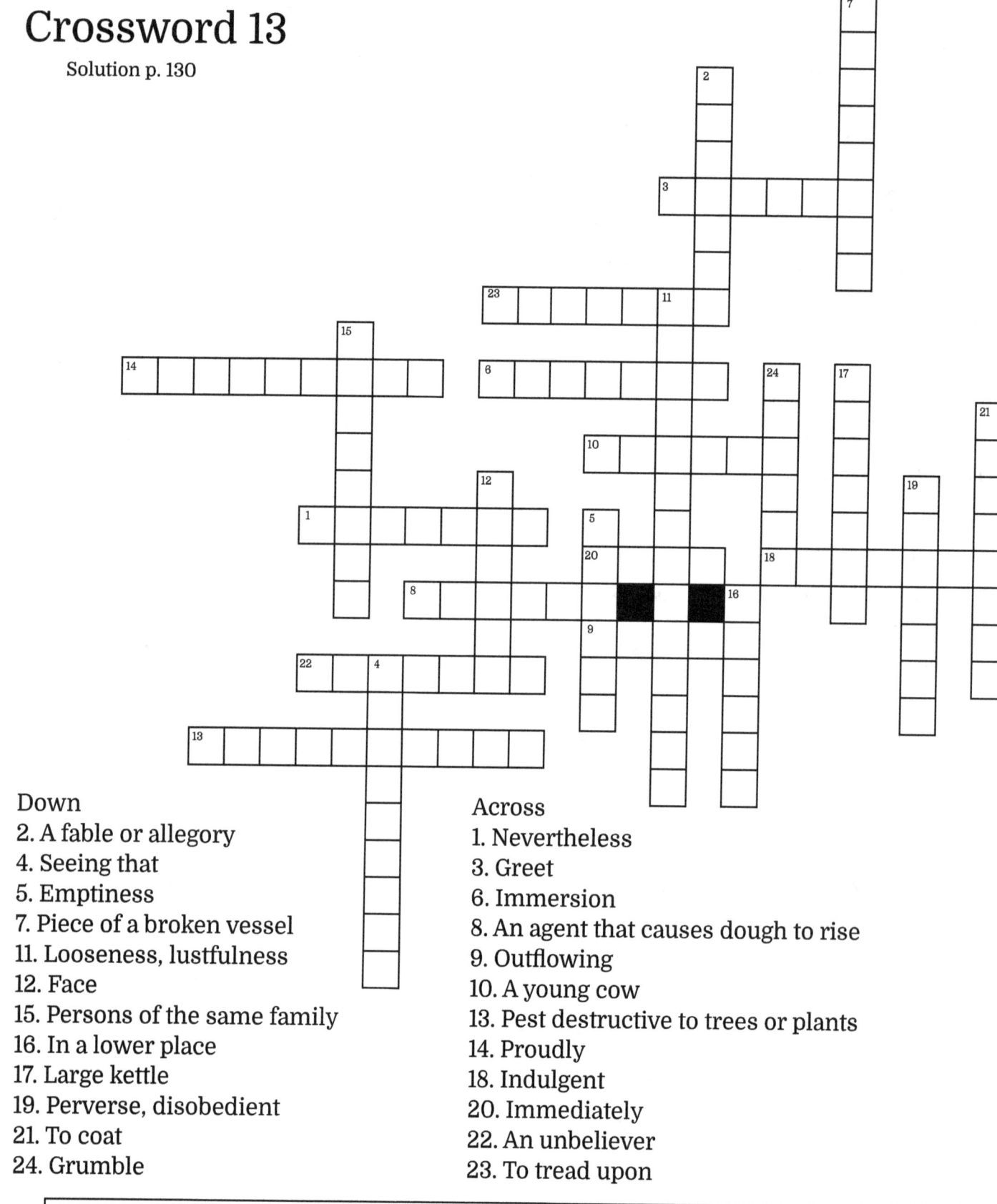

Down
2. A fable or allegory
4. Seeing that
5. Emptiness
7. Piece of a broken vessel
11. Looseness, lustfulness
12. Face
15. Persons of the same family
16. In a lower place
17. Large kettle
19. Perverse, disobedient
21. To coat
24. Grumble

Across
1. Nevertheless
3. Greet
6. Immersion
8. An agent that causes dough to rise
9. Outflowing
10. A young cow
13. Pest destructive to trees or plants
14. Proudly
18. Indulgent
20. Immediately
22. An unbeliever
23. To tread upon

WORD BANK			
ANON	HAUGHTILY	LASCIVIOUSNESS	POTSHERD
BAPTISM	HEIFER	LEAVEN	RIOTOUS
CALDRON	HOWBEIT	MURMUR	SALUTE
CANKERWORM	INFIDEL	NETHER	TRAMPLE
FORSOMUCH	ISSUE	PARABLE	VANITY
FROWARD	KINSFOLK	PLAISTER	VISAGE

Fill in the Blank - Titus Chapter 1

Use the definitions in parentheses to select the words that belong in the text and write them in the blanks. Check your answers in your Bible.

⁶ If any be blameless, the husband of one wife, having faithful children not accused of (uproar) _____ or unruly.⁷ For a bishop must be blameless, as the (minister) _____ of God; not selfwilled, not soon angry, not given to wine, no striker, not given to filthy (profit) _____; ⁸ But a lover of (receiving guests) _____, a lover of good men, (serious) _____, just, holy, (self-controlled) _____; ⁹ Holding fast the faithful word as he hath been taught, that he may be able by sound (truths of the gospel) _____ both to (encourage to good) _____ and to (prove guilty) _____ the (contradictors) _____. ¹⁰ For there are many (disobedient) _____ and vain talkers and deceivers, specially they of the circumcision: ¹¹ Whose mouths must be stopped, who (corrupt) _____whole houses, teaching things which they ought not, for filthy lucre's sake. ¹² One of themselves, even a (foreteller of future events) _____of their own, said, the Cretians are alway liars, evil beasts, slow bellies. ¹³ This witness is true. Wherefore (reprove) _____ them sharply, that they may be sound in the faith; ¹⁴ Not giving heed to Jewish (made-up tales) _____, and commandments of men, that turn from the truth. ¹⁵ Unto the pure all things are pure: but unto them that are defiled and unbelieving is nothing pure; but even their mind and (judgment of right and wrong) _____ is (made dirty) _____. ¹⁶ They (declare) _____ that they know God; but in works they deny him, being (very hateful) _____, and disobedient, and unto every good work (abandoned to sin) _____.

ABOMINABLE	GAINSAYERS	RIOT
CONSCIENCE	HOSPITALITY	SOBER
CONVINCE	LUCRE	STEWARD
DEFILED	PROFESS	SUBVERT
DOCTRINE	PROPHET	TEMPERATE
EXHORT	REBUKE	UNRULY
FABLES	REPROBATE	

Snowflakes #4

Solution p. 123

Select a word from the word bank for each numbered clue and write it across the snowflake. When you have filled in all the answers, some of the letters on the edges will spell a word from the Bible. Write each letter on its corresponding number to reveal the word.

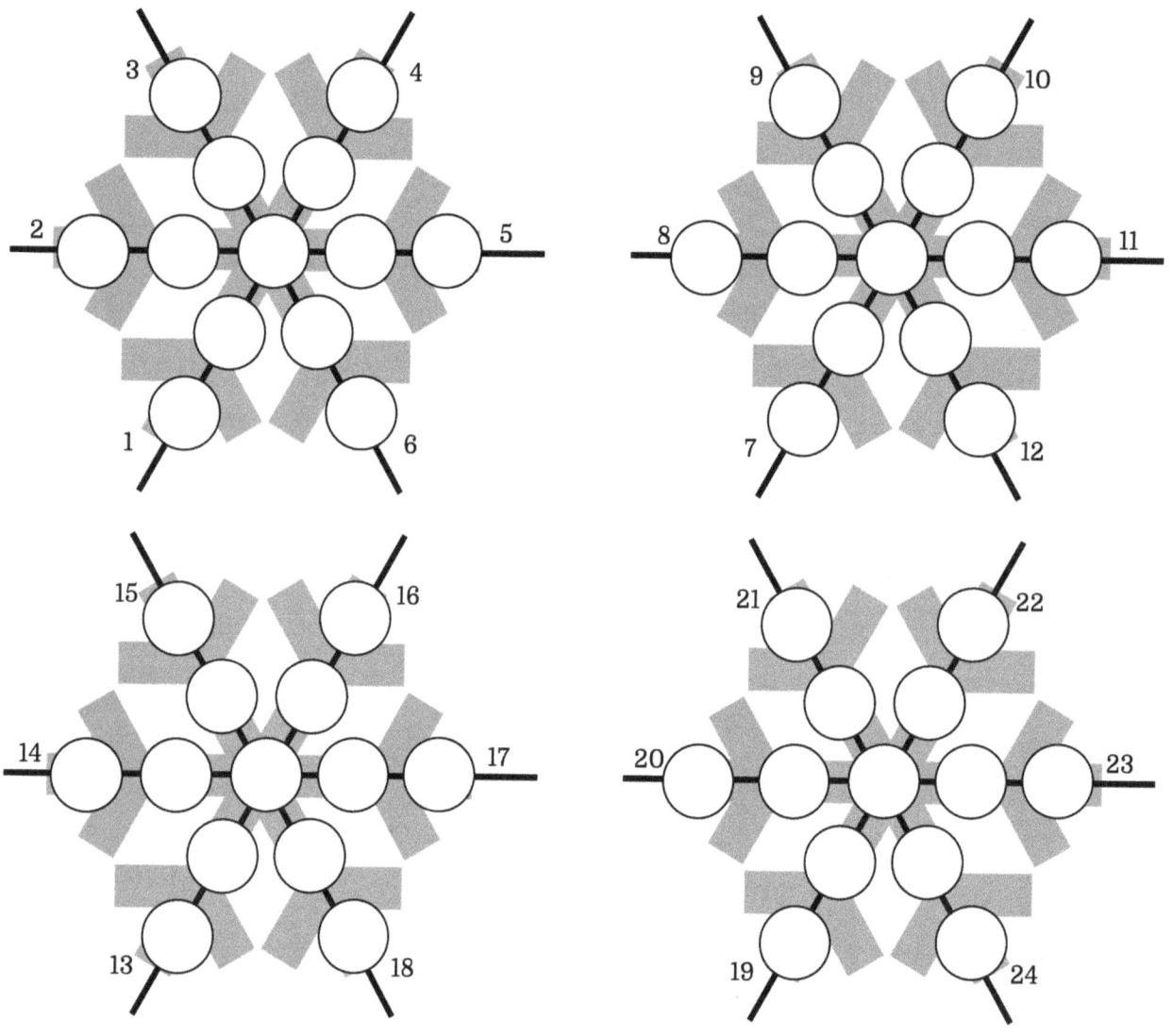

1. A rude or surly person
2. Interest paid on a loan
3. Bed
7. Hebrew dry measure
8. Apron worn by the high priest
9. To despise or neglect

13. Hard lumps of earth
14. Scent
15. The race or line of a family
19. A house built of sticks for temporary use
20. Angry
21. Proud

Word Bank

ABHOR	CHURL	COUCH	EPHOD	STOCK	USURY
BOOTH	CLODS	EPHAH	ODOUR	STOUT	WROTH

8-Letter word from 2 Kings 12:7 _ _ _ _ _ _ _ _
19 17 8 9 1 6 7 21

Compound Words #2

Match the two parts of each compound word using the definition. Write the letter of the second half in the blank space following the first half.   Solution p. 123

1. Bar on which wheels turn =	AXLE	+ _____		A. BITTEN
2. A privilege resulting from descent =	BIRTH	+ _____		B. BREADTH
3. Female slave =	BOND	+ _____		C. COTE
4. Armor for the chest =	BREAST	+ _____		D. DISHES
5. Sulphur =	BRIM	+ _____		E. FAT
6. Sellers =	CHAP	+ _____		F. FROST
7. Mediator =	DAYS	+ _____		G. GLASS
8. Porter =	DOOR	+ _____		H. GOAT
9. Making contrary statements =	DOUBLE	+ _____		I. HOOK
10. Instrument used to pull meat out of a pot =	FLESH	+ _____		J. KEEPER
11. To caution beforehand =	FORE	+ _____		K. KINDNESS
12. First in place =	FORE	+ _____		L. LIVE
13. Having four sides and four angles equal =	FOUR	+ _____		M. MAID
14. Voluntary =	FREE	+ _____		N. MAN
15. Space equal to the width of a palm =	HAND	+ _____		O. MEN
16. Product of manual labor =	HANDY	+ _____		P. MONGER
17. White particles of ice =	HOAR	+ _____		Q. MOST
18. Weakened by hunger =	HUNGER	+ _____		R. PLATE
19. Mirror =	LOOKING	+ _____		S. PLUS
20. Tender regard =	LOVING	+ _____		T. RIGHT
21. Those who kidnap and sell people =	MEN	+ _____		U. SPRING
22. Staff used to measure =	METE	+ _____		V. SQUARE
23. Descendants =	OFF	+ _____		W. STEALERS
24. To survive longer than =	OVER	+ _____		X. STONE
25. Superabundance =	OVER	+ _____		Y. TONGUED
26. Animal sent into the wilderness bearing sin =	SCAPE	+ _____		Z. TREE
27. Small inclosure for sheep =	SHEEP	+ _____		AA. WARN
28. Places to put trimmed burnt wicks =	SNUFF	+ _____		BB. WILL
29. Man who commits sexual sin =	WHORE	+ _____		CC. WORK
30. Trough beneath a grape press =	WINE	+ _____		DD. YARD

Down the Stairs #4

Use the definitions to place words from the word bank into each row. One letter is given in each word.

Solution p. 122

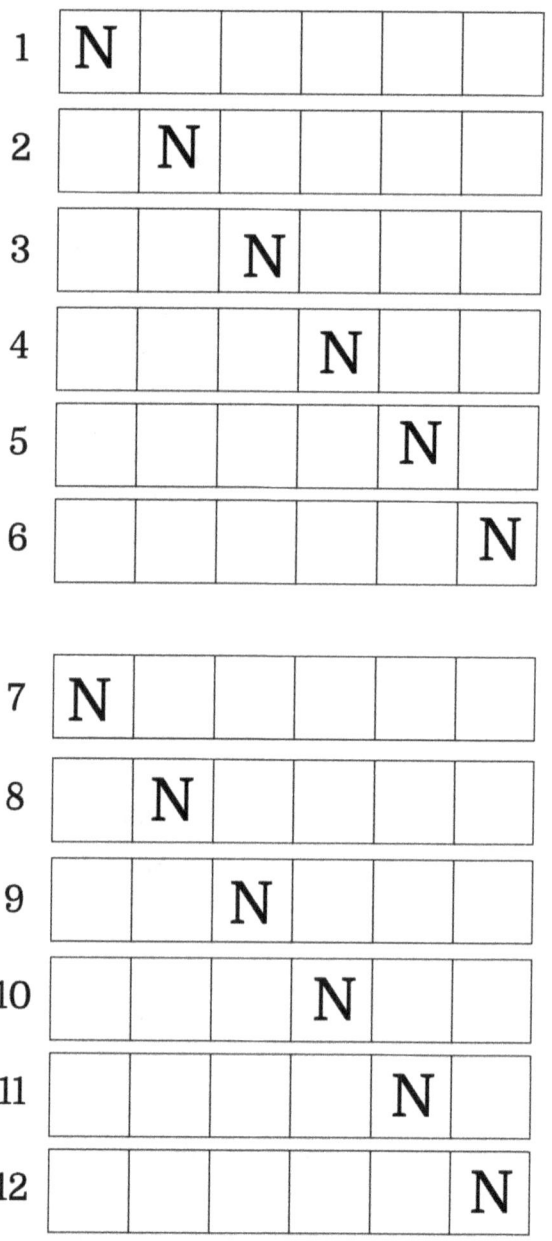

Word Bank

ABOUND
ANOINT
BIDDEN
ENDUED
ENDURE
ENMITY
FAMINE
GARNER
GENDER
MOLTEN
NETHER
NOBLES
NOUGHT
NOVICE
OFFEND
SIGNET
SODDEN
STANCH
SUNDER
TALENT
THONGS
VANITY
WANTON
YONDER

1. New convert
2. To smear or pour over with a substance
3. To beget
4. Stop the flow of blood
5. Hebrew coin
6. Loose, lewd
7. In a lower place
8. Supplied
9. Emptiness
10. Straps of leather
11. Scarcity of food
12. Boiled

13. Nothing
14. Ill will
15. In two pieces
16. Storehouse for grain
17. To be in great plenty
18. Made of melted metal
19. People of honorable family
20. Bear
21. At a distance within view
22. A seal
23. Displease
24. Invited

78

A to Z #4

Solution p. 121

The answer to each lettered clue will contain its corresponding letter **somewhere** in the word. Select carefully from the word bank!

A. At a distance
B. That which makes difficult
C. Cutting off
D. Disheartened
E. Diverted from its original purpose
F. Terrify
G. Harvest
H. Raised
I. Contention
J. Every 50th year
K. Parting by violence
L. Keeping out of sight
M. Carpenter's tool for determining a horizontal line
N. Avoided
O. Opportunity
P. One who foretells the future by observing signs
Q. Living
R. Skilled craftsman
S. Subside or lessen
T. Covenant
U. Canal for the conveyance of water
V. Food prepared for human use
W. Noncompliance; disobedience
X. Being at an end
Y. Irreverent words against God
Z. Warmly engaged in the pursuit of an object

Word Bank

AFFRIGHT	HOISED
ALOOF	INGATHERING
ARTIFICER	JUBILE
ASSWAGE	LURKING
BLASPHEMY	OCCASION
BREAKINGS	PLUMMET
CONCISION	PROGNOSTICATOR
CONDUIT	QUICK
CUMBRANCE	SHUNNED
DISMAYED	STRIVINGS
ESTRANGED	TESTAMENT
EXTINCT	VICTUALS
FROWARDNESS	ZEALOUS

A _____
B _____
C _____
D _____
E _____
F _____
G _____
H _____
I _____
J _____
K _____
L _____
M _____
N _____
O _____
P _____
Q _____
R _____
S _____
T _____
U _____
V _____
W _____
X _____
Y _____
Z _____

Crossword 14

Solution p. 130

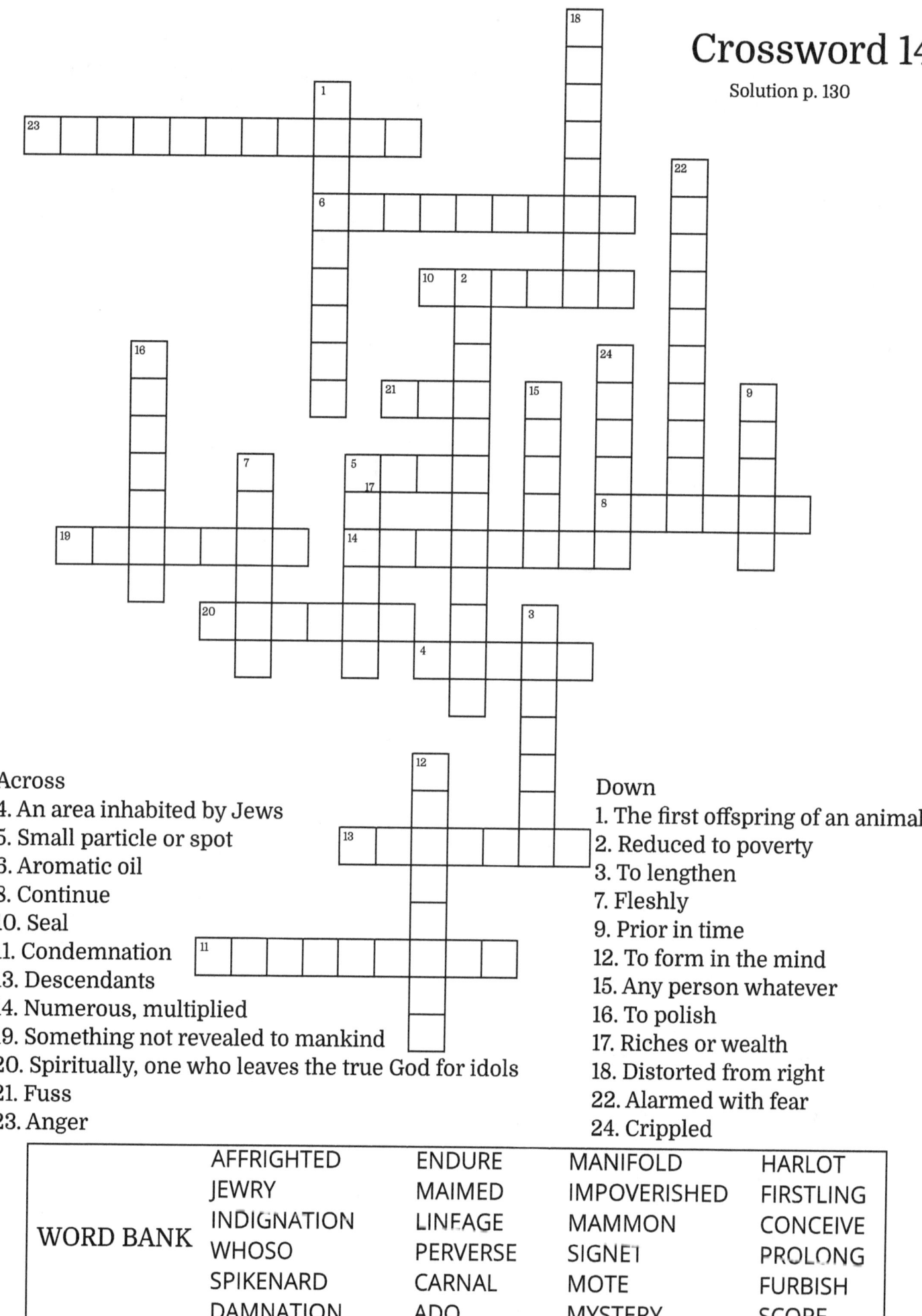

Across

4. An area inhabited by Jews
5. Small particle or spot
6. Aromatic oil
8. Continue
10. Seal
11. Condemnation
13. Descendants
14. Numerous, multiplied
19. Something not revealed to mankind
20. Spiritually, one who leaves the true God for idols
21. Fuss
23. Anger

Down

1. The first offspring of an animal
2. Reduced to poverty
3. To lengthen
7. Fleshly
9. Prior in time
12. To form in the mind
15. Any person whatever
16. To polish
17. Riches or wealth
18. Distorted from right
22. Alarmed with fear
24. Crippled

WORD BANK			
AFFRIGHTED	ENDURE	MANIFOLD	HARLOT
JEWRY	MAIMED	IMPOVERISHED	FIRSTLING
INDIGNATION	LINEAGE	MAMMON	CONCEIVE
WHOSO	PERVERSE	SIGNET	PROLONG
SPIKENARD	CARNAL	MOTE	FURBISH
DAMNATION	ADO	MYSTERY	SCORE

Secret Word #4

Solution p. 124

Place a word from the box below on each line. The circled letters in each puzzle will spell out a secret word also found in the box (and in the Bible).

Small bottle

Think

Throw

Except

Secret Word: _____

Pine resin

Middle

To hate

Reverence

Secret Word: _____

Weep loudly

Splendor

Group united by belief

Rooster

Secret Word: _____

Strike

Not defective

Belonging to thee

Urge or constrain

Secret Word: _____

Longing desire

Kill

Food of any kind

To vomit

Secret Word: _____

Branch of a tree

Where Hebrews live

Made an oath

Venomous snake

Secret Word: _____

ADDER	LAMP	MIDST	PRESS	SPUE
BEAR	LOCK	MOTE	SAVE	SWARE
BOUGH	LOSE	PIETY	SECT	THINE
CAST	LOTHE	PITCH	SLAY	TROW
COCK	LUST	PITY	SMITE	VIAL
JEWRY	MEAT	POMP	SOUND	WAIL

Synonym Scramble 4

Each set of scrambled words has a common meaning.
Use the definition as a hint.

Solution p. 126

Riches or wealth

UCLER   = _ _ _ _ _ _ _ _ _ _   IAGN   = _ _ _ _ _ _ _ _ _ _

ERPRSYITOP   = _ _ _ _ _ _ _ _ _ _   MMMANO   = _ _ _ _ _ _ _ _ _ _

A representation with the same appearance

MILISDIUET   = _ _ _ _ _ _ _ _ _ _   EBSEACLREMN   = _ _ _ _ _ _ _ _ _ _

KISSEELN   = _ _ _ _ _ _ _ _ _ _   GIAEM   = _ _ _ _ _ _ _ _ _ _

Appropriate

YLCMEO   = _ _ _ _ _ _ _ _ _ _   TENNENCIOV   = _ _ _ _ _ _ _ _ _ _

TMEE   = _ _ _ _ _ _ _ _ _ _   MYSEEL   = _ _ _ _ _ _ _ _ _ _

Right away, at once

NNAO   = _ _ _ _ _ _ _ _ _ _   IHOTFRTWH   = _ _ _ _ _ _ _ _ _ _

WHISGRAATTY   = _ _ _ _ _ _ _ _ _ _   TILEMMEIADY   = _ _ _ _ _ _ _ _ _ _

To repay either good or evil

UETEQRI   = _ _ _ _ _ _ _ _ _ _   EOCERPMENS   = _ _ _ _ _ _ _ _ _ _

NAVGEE   = _ _ _ _ _ _ _ _ _ _   RTAILETAE   = _ _ _ _ _ _ _ _ _ _

Request

CPTLUPAIISNO   = _ _ _ _ _ _ _ _ _ _   ENARTITY   = _ _ _ _ _ _ _ _ _ _

EOTNTIPI   = _ _ _ _ _ _ _ _ _ _   EPYARR   = _ _ _ _ _ _ _ _ _ _

Snowflakes #5

Solution p. 123

Select a word from the word bank for each numbered clue and write it across the snowflake. When you have filled in all the answers, some of the letters on the edges will spell a word from the Bible. Write each letter on its corresponding number to reveal the word.

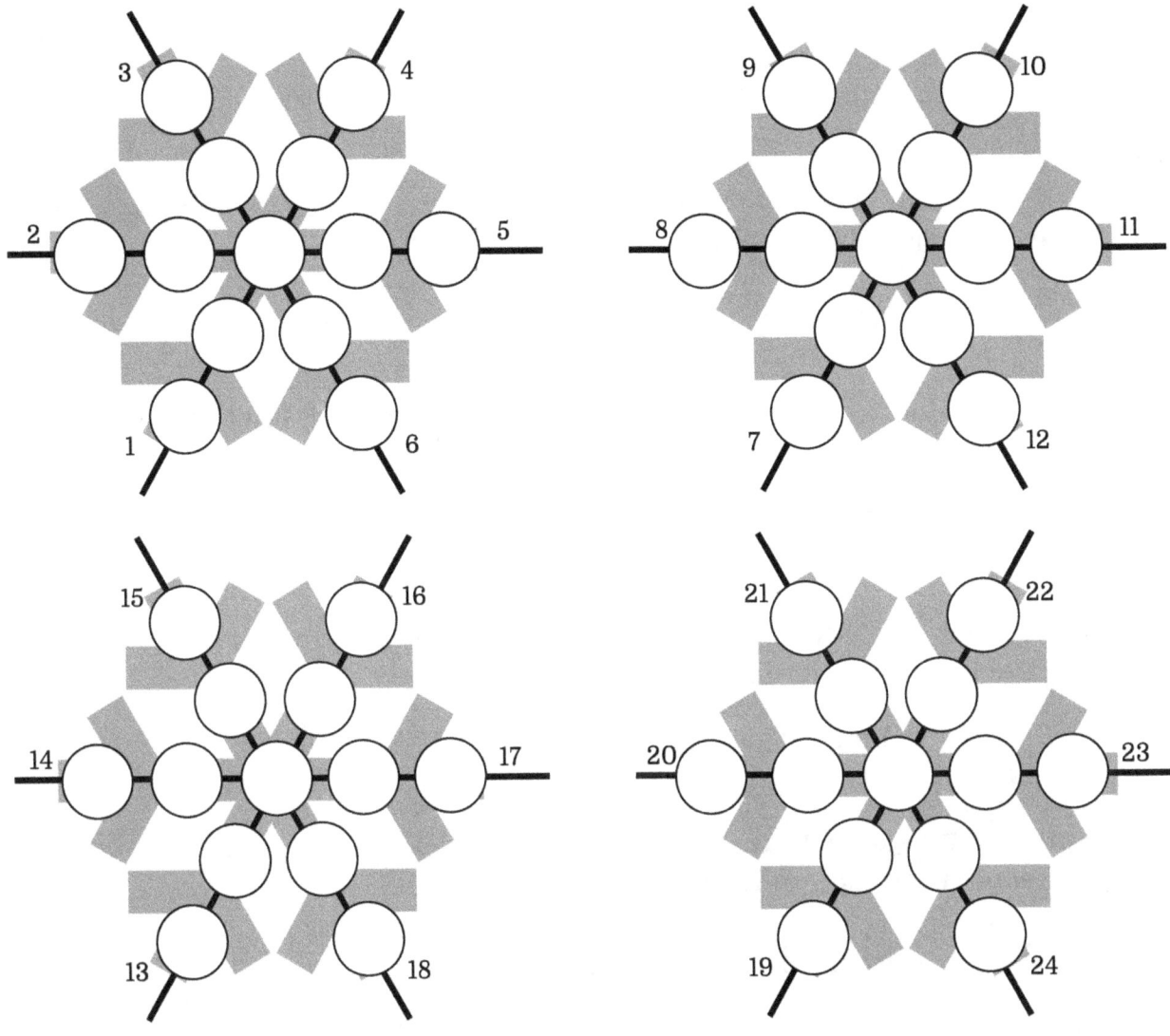

1. To correct
2. A crack or crevice
3. A broad piece of cloth
7. Surrender
8. Place
9. Distort or twist

13. To instruct in faith
14. The region of the hips and groin
15. The inward parts, the heart
19. Pale green gemstone
20. Goods for sale
21. Danger

Word Bank

AMEND	CLEFT	LOINS	REINS	STEAD	WREST
BERYL	EDIFY	PERIL	SHEET	WARES	YIELD

8-Letter word from Psalm 33:2 _ _ _ _ _ _ _ _
                               21 8 1 22 6 13 15 7

Which Word?

Which of the words with similar meaning belongs in each verse? Circle your answer. Check your answers in your Bible.

Proverbs 9:8

_____ not a scorner, lest he hate thee: rebuke a wise man, and he will love thee.

        Reproach   Reprove   Upbraid

2 Chronicles 15:11

And they offered unto the Lord the same time, of the _____ which they had brought, seven hundred oxen and seven thousand sheep.

        Plunder   Prey   Spoil

Isaiah 2:11

The _____ looks of man shall be humbled, and the haughtiness of men shall be bowed down, and the Lord alone shall be exalted in that day.

        Stately   Eminent   Lofty

Acts 13:26

Men and brethren, children of the _____ of Abraham, and whosoever among you feareth God, to you is the word of this salvation sent.

        Lineage   Posterity   Stock

Titus 1:15

Unto the pure all things are pure: but unto them that are _____and unbelieving is nothing pure; but even their mind and conscience is _____.

        Corrupted   Defiled   Polluted

2 Peter 3:7

But the heavens and the earth, which are now, by the same word are kept in store, reserved unto fire against the day of judgment and _____ of ungodly men.

        Condemnation   Damnation   Perdition

Romans 13:13

Let us walk honestly, as in the day; not in rioting and drunkenness, not in chambering and wantonness, not in _____ and envying.

        Contention   Emulation   Strife

2 Kings 13:18

And he said, Take the arrows. And he took them. And he said unto the king of Israel, Smite upon the ground. And he smote thrice, and _____.

        Ceased   Halted   Stayed

Crossword 15

Solution p. 130

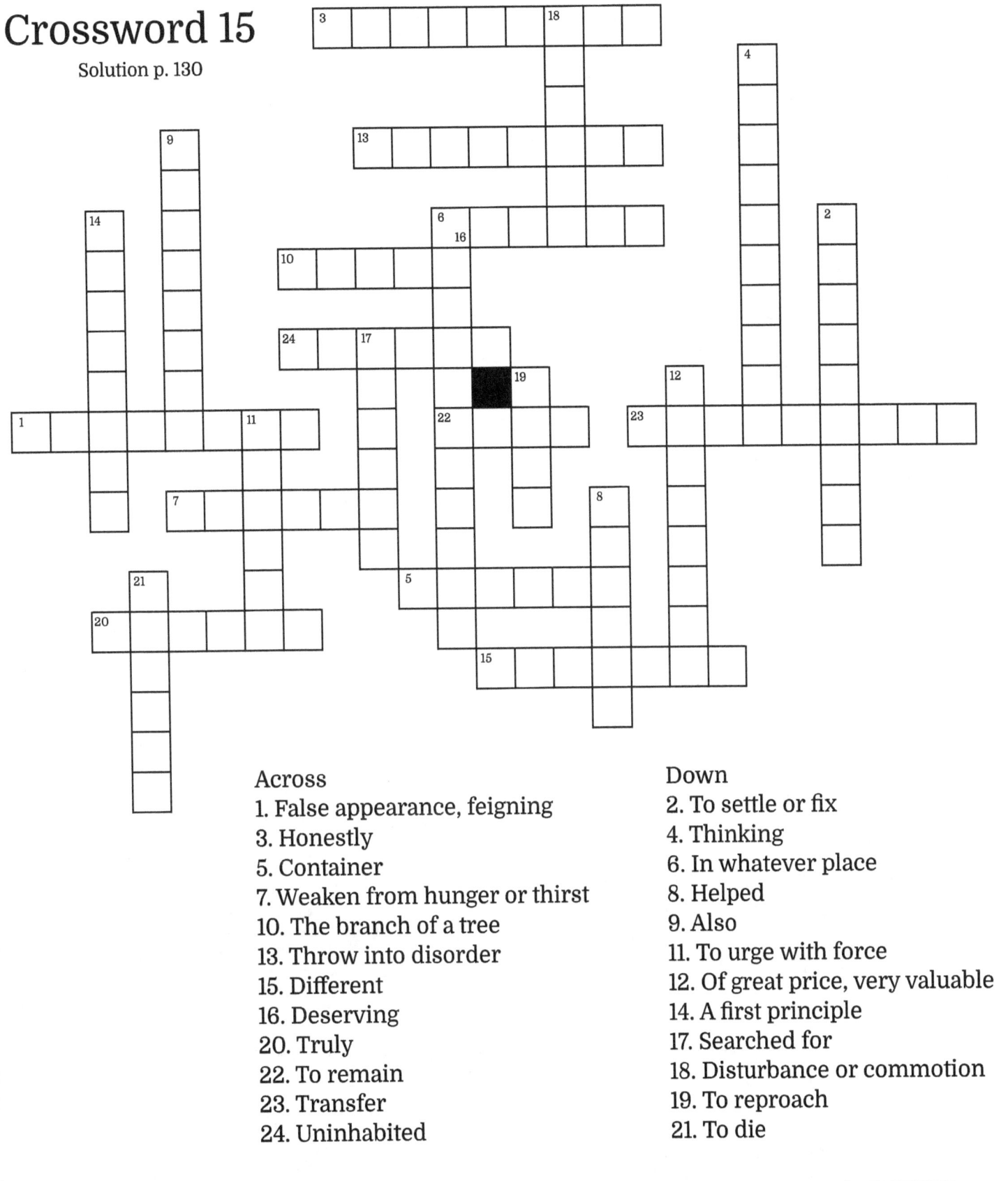

Across
1. False appearance, feigning
3. Honestly
5. Container
7. Weaken from hunger or thirst
10. The branch of a tree
13. Throw into disorder
15. Different
16. Deserving
20. Truly
22. To remain
23. Transfer
24. Uninhabited

Down
2. To settle or fix
4. Thinking
6. In whatever place
8. Helped
9. Also
11. To urge with force
12. Of great price, very valuable
14. A first principle
17. Searched for
18. Disturbance or commotion
19. To reproach
21. To die

WORD BANK

BOUGH	ESTABLISH	PRETENCE	TUMULT
COGITATION	FAMISH	RAIL	UPRIGHTLY
COMPEL	HOLPEN	RUDIMENT	VERILY
CONFOUND	LIKEWISE	SOUGHT	VESSEL
DESERT	PERISH	STAY	WHERESOEVER
DIVERSE	PRECIOUS	TRANSLATE	WORTHY

Select-A-Syllable #5

Each of the answers to the following clues is made up of two syllables that can be found in the box. Put them together and write your completed words in the spaces provided. The numbers in parentheses indicate the total number of letters in each answer. Each syllable will be used only once.

Solution p. 121

1. Flat open country (9)   _____
2. Grape harvest (7)   _____
3. The first offspring of an animal (9)   _____
4. Meeting (9)   _____
5. Travel (7)   _____
6. Break the law (10)   _____
7. Pagan, idol worshipper (7)   _____
8. A kind of trumpet (7)   _____
9. Small movable window (8)   _____
10. Internal (6)   _____
11. Carving (7)   _____
12. Place of receiving (7)   _____
13. Make intimately known (8)   _____
14. Entrance (9)   _____
15. Residue, that which is left after removal of a part (7)   _____
16. News (7)   _____
17. Bands worn on the forehead (9)   _____
18. Vigilant (7)   _____
19. Armor (7)   _____
20. Pillow (7)   _____

Syllable Box

AC	EN	ING	NESS	SACK
BOL	FIRST	INGS	NEY	STER
BUT	FRONT	JEAL	OLD	TAGE
CASE	GRAV	JOUR	OUS	THRESH
CEIPT	GRESS	LETS	PAIGN	TID
CHAM	HAR	LING	QUAINT	TRANS
CON	HEATH	MENT	RE	VIN
COURSE	IN	NANT	REM	WARD

Caterpillars #2

Use the definitions to place words from the word bank into each caterpillar. The letter at the end of one word will be the starting letter of the next word. Words may run across, up or down, but not backwards.

Solution p. 132

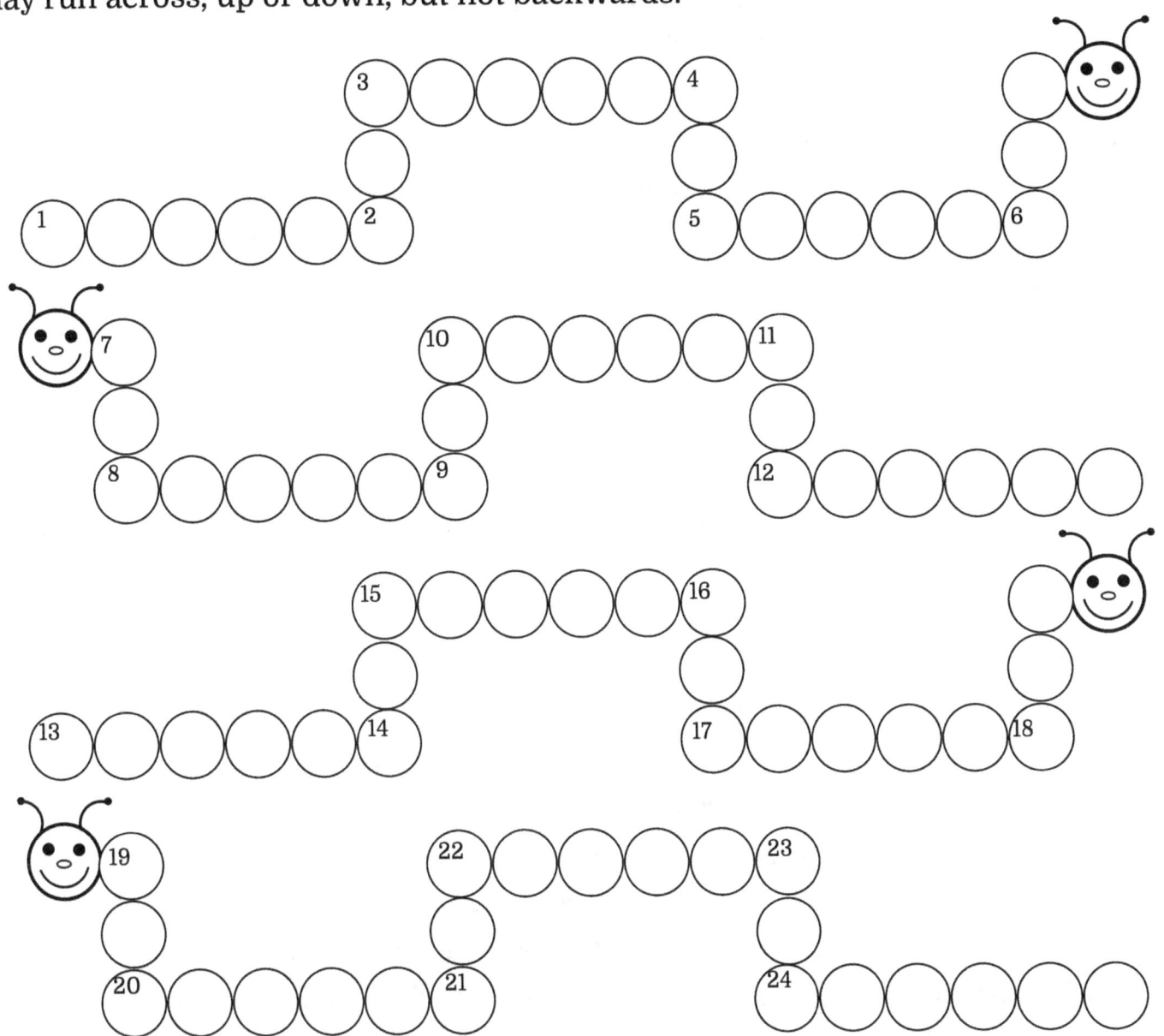

1. Container
2. Boy
3. To drop
4. To allow or permit
5. Deserving confidence
6. Plural second person pronoun
7. Tool used to pierce holes
8. Alliance
9. To plow
10. Severity
11. Male sheep
12. To intrude into others' business

13. Prevent decay of a dead body
14. To injure
15. A tumor on the body
16. Past tense of got
17. Small defensive shield
18. Belonging to thee
19. Qualified
20. Small flat surface
21. Broken part of flax
22. To separate chaff from grain
23. To know
24. To push or drive with force

APT	RIGOUR
AUL	RISING
DISTIL	TABLET
EAR	TARGET
EMBALM	THRUST
GAT	THY
LAD	TOW
LEAGUE	TRUSTY
LET	VESSEL
MAR	WINNOW
MEDDLE	WIT
RAM	YOU

Fill in the Blank from 2 Corinthians 9:5-15

Use the definitions in parentheses to select the words that belong in the text and write them in the blanks. Check your answers in your Bible.

⁵ Therefore I thought it necessary to (incite by words)_____ the brethren, that they would go before unto you, and make up beforehand your (something given generously)_____, whereof ye had notice before, that the same might be ready, as a matter of bounty, and not as of (desire to obtain, in a bad sense) _____. ⁶ But this I say, He which soweth (frugally)_____shall reap also (frugally)_____; and he which soweth (liberally)_____ shall reap also (liberally)_____. ⁷ Every man according as he purposeth in his heart, so let him give; not (unwillingly)_____, or of necessity: for God loveth a cheerful giver. ⁸ And God is able to make all grace abound toward you; that ye, always having all (adequate ability)_____in all things, may (have in great plenty)_____ to every good work: ⁹ [As it is written, He hath (scattered)_____ abroad; he hath given to the poor: his righteousness remaineth for ever. ¹⁰ Now he that (supplies)_____ seed to the sower both minister bread for your food, and multiply your seed sown, and increase the fruits of your righteousness;] ¹¹ Being enriched in every thing to all (generosity in giving) _____, which causeth through us thanksgiving to God. ¹² For the (distribution)_____ of this service not only supplieth the want of the saints, but is abundant also by many thanksgivings unto God; ¹³ Whiles by the experiment of this (service)_____ they glorify God for your professed subjection unto the gospel of Christ, and for your (generous) _____ distribution unto them, and unto all men; ¹⁴ And by their prayer for you, which long after you for the exceeding grace of God in you. ¹⁵ Thanks be unto God for his unspeakable gift.

ABOUND	COVETOUSNESS	SPARINGLY
ADMINISTRATION	DISPERSED	SUFFICIENCY
BOUNTIFULLY	EXHORT	MINISTERETH
BOUNTIFULNESS	GRUDGINGLY	MINISTRATION
BOUNTY	LIBERAL	

Secret Word #5

Solution p. 124

Place a word from the box below on each line. The circled letters in each puzzle will spell out a secret word also found in the box (and in the Bible).

Puzzle 1 (left)

Aquatic plant

Fever

Lights

To rescue

Secret Word: _____

Puzzle 2 (right)

Growing vigorously

Move side-to-side

Count

Guard

Secret Word: _____

Puzzle 3 (left)

To blow in scorn

Medicinal plant

Dish of food

Empty

Secret Word: _____

Puzzle 4 (right)

Low place between hills

Small insects

Marshes

Portion

Secret Word: _____

Puzzle 5 (left)

A weight of measure

Lengthwise fabric threads

Greatly

Low

Secret Word: _____

Puzzle 6 (right)

To peel

Sore swelling on the body

Handle

Lain

Secret Word: _____

AGUE	FENS	LIFE	RANK	SORE
ALOE	HAFT	MESS	RASE	TALE
BOIL	LEAN	NEAR	REEL	URIM
DALE	LICE	PILL	RUSH	VAIN
DEAL	LIED	PLEA	SAME	WARD
DRAM	LIEN	PUFF	SAVE	WARP

89

Crossword 16

Solution p. 130

Across

2. Force by which something is taken from a person
6. Wanting food
7. Surface used for sacrifice or worship
8. A heap of manure
9. Free from pollution
11. Justice, right
14. Strike
18. Heroic acts
19. Not carelessly
20. To count
21. Interwoven
23. Condition of any person or thing

Down

1. Unable to be counted
3. To flee from, to shun
4. Iota
5. To which
10. Hebrew coin
12. To surround with enemy troops
13. Distort or twist
15. Distress
16. A structure made of parts joined together
17. Account
22. Asking earnestly and humbly
24. Intricate

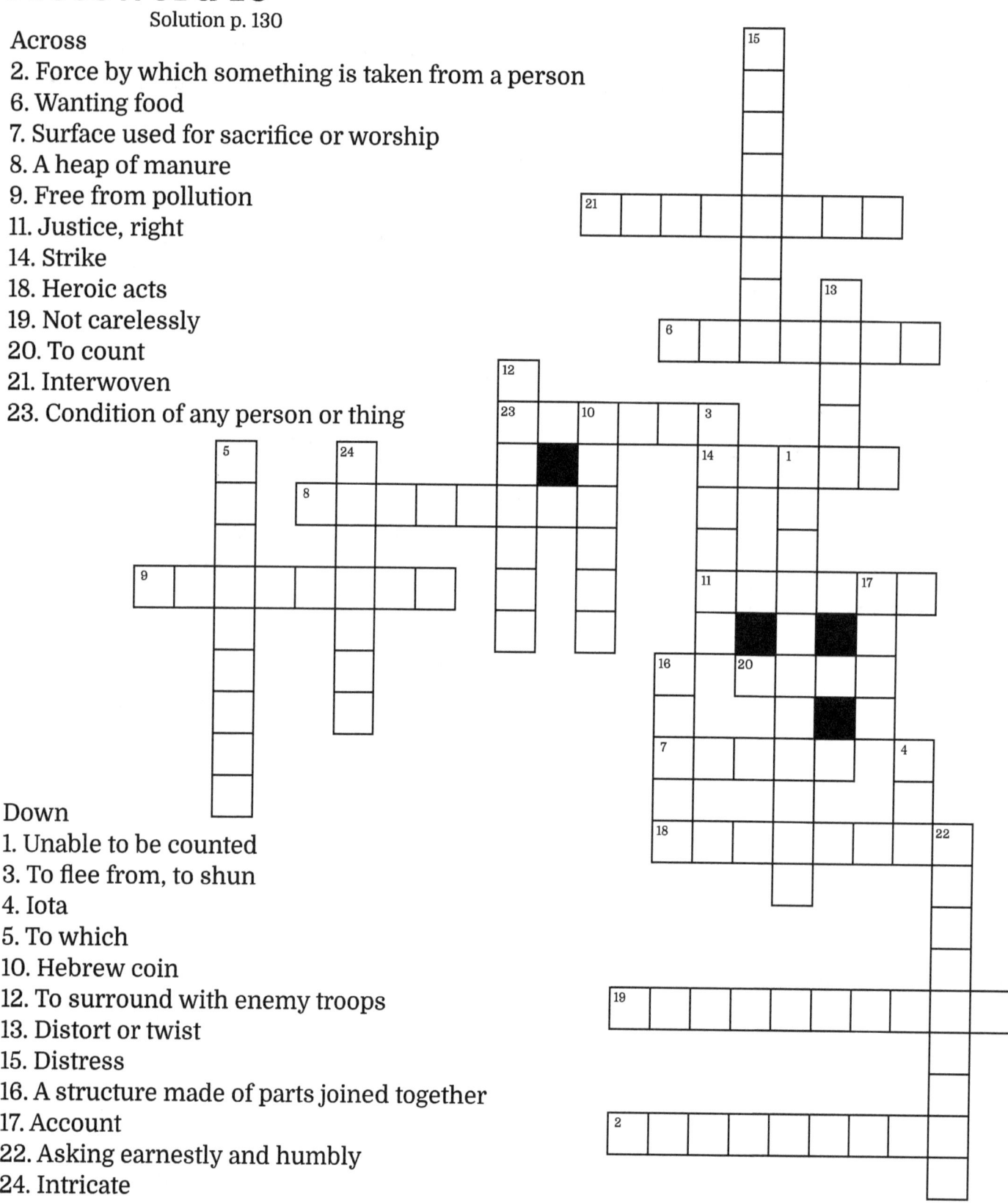

WORD BANK	ALTAR	ESCHEW	INNUMERABLE	TALENT
	BESIEGE	ESTATE	JOT	TELL
	CURIOUS	EXPLOITS	PURIFIED	VEXATION
	DILIGENTLY	EXTORTION	SMITE	WHEREUNTO
	DUNGHILL	FRAME	SUPPLIANT	WREATHEN
	EQUITY	HUNGRED	TALE	WREST

Finish the Word #6

All of these nouns have the same ending. Can you finish them, using the definitions and word list?
The number of blanks indicates the number of missing letters.

Definition	Answer	Word List
Illegal taking by force or duress	_ _ _ _ _ _TION	COMMOTION
Disorder	_ _ _ _ _ _TION	CONFIRMATION
Condemnation	_ _ _ _ _ _TION	CONFISCATION
Strife; competition	_ _ _ _ _ _TION	CONTENTION
Restraint of passions	_ _ _ _ _ _ _TION	CONVOCATION
Strife; debate	_ _ _ _ _ _ _TION	DAMNATION
Calculation of value	_ _ _ _ _ _ _TION	DECLARATION
Deliverance	_ _ _ _ _ _ _TION	DISCRETION
Good judgment; prudence	_ _ _ _ _ _ _TION	DISPENSATION
Being under the power of another	_ _ _ _ _ _ _TION	DISPUTATION
Amendment	_ _ _ _ _ _ _ _TION	EMULATION
God-breathed	_ _ _ _ _ _ _ _TION	ESTIMATION
Removing from one place to another	_ _ _ _ _ _ _ _TION	EXHORTATION
Proclamation	_ _ _ _ _ _ _ _TION	EXTORTION
Anything that excites anger	_ _ _ _ _ _ _ _TION	IMAGINATION
Anger	_ _ _ _ _ _ _ _TION	INDIGNATION
Argument; controversy	_ _ _ _ _ _ _ _TION	INSPIRATION
Making good for loss, damage, or injury	_ _ _ _ _ _ _ _ _TION	MINISTRATION
Severe distress	_ _ _ _ _ _ _ _ _TION	MODERATION
Idea of the mind	_ _ _ _ _ _ _ _ _TION	PROPITIATION
Assembly	_ _ _ _ _ _ _ _ _TION	PROVOCATION
Encouragement to do good	_ _ _ _ _ _ _ _ _TION	PURIFICATION
Atoning sacrifice	_ _ _ _ _ _ _ _ _TION	REDEMPTION
Seizure of goods by authorities	_ _ _ _ _ _ _ _ _TION	REFORMATION
Payment	_ _ _ _ _ _ _ _ _TION	RESTITUTION
Distribution	_ _ _ _ _ _ _ _ _TION	SATISFACTION
Service	_ _ _ _ _ _ _ _ _TION	SUBJECTION
Establishment	_ _ _ _ _ _ _ _ _TION	TRANSLATION
Cleansing	_ _ _ _ _ _ _ _ _TION	TRIBULATION

Solution p. 120

Anagrams #5

Each word set is an anagram of a single Bible word. Use the definition to unscramble them. Stumped? Use the reference verse for help.   Solution p. 125

Example: Owing something to someone   bend diet   __indebted__

1. Apart; into parts (Mark 10:9)   dear sun   _____
2. Immersion (Luke 7:29)   spam bit   _____
3. Inflamed (Leviticus 13:25)   grub inn   _____
4. Bounced or rocked (Isaiah 66:12)   dad lend   _____
5. Troops stationed in a town (1 Samuel 13:3)   sonar rig   _____
6. Imagination (Ezekiel 8:12)   airy gem   _____
7. Contagious skin disease (Deuteronomy 24:8)   spy lore   _____
8. Softened (Isaiah 1:6)   limo field   _____
9. Affliction (Job 5:21)   sure cog   _____
10. Brave (1 Samuel 16:18)   lava tin   _____
11. Effected, produced (Numbers 23:23)   grow hut   _____
12. Abominable (Ezekiel 11:21)   salted beet   _____
13. Trick (Ephesians 4:14)   this leg   _____
14. Period of rest (Exodus 8:15)   tip seer   _____
15. To subdue or restrain (Colossians 3:5)   toy firm   _____
16. Dominion (Daniel 6:24)   may rest   _____
17. Educated (Isaiah 29:11)   real end   _____
18. Wanting food (Matthew 12:1)   nerd hug   _____
19. To lose by offense or fault (Ezra 10:8)   offer it   _____
20. Lack of rain or water (Deuteronomy 8:15)   hot drug   _____
21. Sharp edge of a plow (1 Samuel 13:20)   curl toe   _____
22. Slavery (Exodus 6:5)   ego band   _____
23. To attribute (1 Samuel 18:8)   rib case   _____

Sort Them Out #3

Write each word under the correct category. Each answer will be used only once.

Solution p. 120

Bulrush Homer Teil

Behemoth Pygarg

Sardine Myrtle Chamois

Mandrake

Span Leviathan

Willow Wormwood Cab

Jasper Nettle Sardius

Shittim

Fathom Chrysolyte

Animals

Plants

Trees

_____

_____

_____

_____

_____

_____

_____

_____

_____

_____

_____

_____

Precious Stones

Measurements

_____

_____

_____

_____

_____

_____

_____

_____

Daisy Chain #2

Beginning at #1 and moving clockwise around the petals, fill in a word from the word bank that matches each definition. On each flower, the last letter of each answer will also be the first letter of the next answer. Solution on p. 132

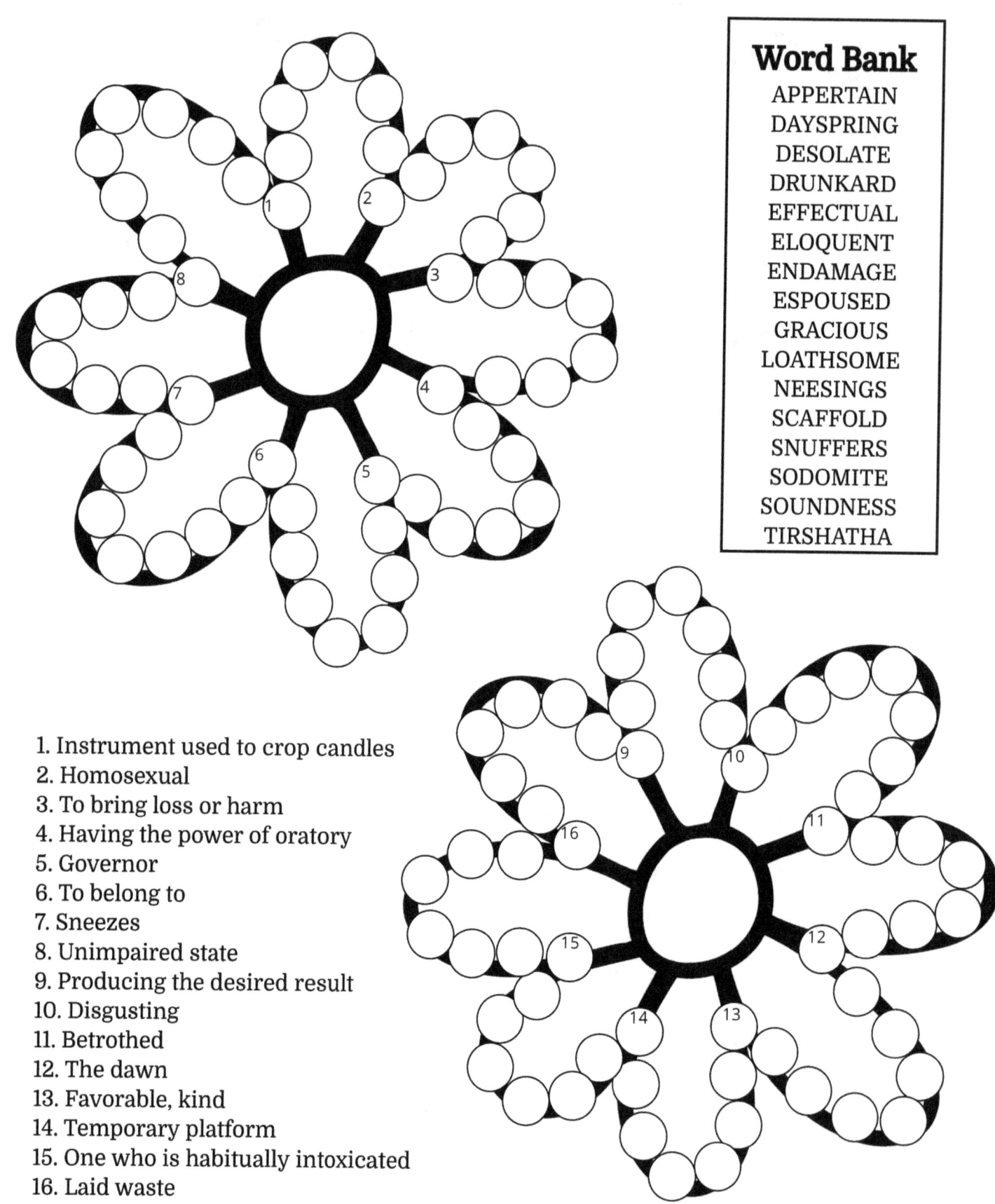

Word Bank

APPERTAIN
DAYSPRING
DESOLATE
DRUNKARD
EFFECTUAL
ELOQUENT
ENDAMAGE
ESPOUSED
GRACIOUS
LOATHSOME
NEESINGS
SCAFFOLD
SNUFFERS
SODOMITE
SOUNDNESS
TIRSHATHA

1. Instrument used to crop candles
2. Homosexual
3. To bring loss or harm
4. Having the power of oratory
5. Governor
6. To belong to
7. Sneezes
8. Unimpaired state
9. Producing the desired result
10. Disgusting
11. Betrothed
12. The dawn
13. Favorable, kind
14. Temporary platform
15. One who is habitually intoxicated
16. Laid waste

94

A to Z #5

Solution p. 121

The answer to each lettered clue will contain its corresponding letter **somewhere** in the word. Select carefully from the word bank!

A. Lovely
B. Despicable people
C. Historic account
D. Drawn in different directions
E. Use of magic arts
F. To a degree that answers the purpose
G. A habitually lazy person
H. Rude or surly
I. To lessen
J. To accept as righteous
K. Tray in which dough is mixed
L. Giving consolation
M. Musician
N. One who converses with departed spirits
O. One who imposes unjust burdens on another
P. In bold defiance of conscience
Q. Pits where stone is dug
R. Forefathers
S. The crime of shedding blood
T. Regard
U. Tasteless
V. Violent, intense
W. Something produced
X. Money spent
Y. A secluded or obscure way
Z. Risked

A	_____
B	_____
C	_____
D	_____
E	_____
F	_____
G	_____
H	_____
I	_____
J	_____
K	_____
L	_____
M	_____
N	_____
O	_____
P	_____
Q	_____
R	_____
S	_____
T	_____
U	_____
V	_____
W	_____
X	_____
Y	_____
Z	_____

Word Bank

ABJECTS	KNEADINGTROUGHS
AMIABLE	MINISH
ATTENDANCE	MINSTREL
BLOODGUILTINESS	NECROMANCER
BYWAY	OPPRESSOR
CHRONICLE	PRESUMPTUOUSLY
CHURLISH	PROGENITORS
COMFORTABLE	QUARRIES
DISTRACTED	SLUGGARD
ENCHANTMENTS	SUFFICIENTLY
EXPENCES	UNSAVOURY
HAZARDED	VEHEMENT
JUSTIFY	WORKMANSHIP

Crossword 17

Solution p. 131

Across
2. To tell in detail
4. Valley
6. Suitable, proper
7. About 1.5 gallons
8. Love excessively
9. A small piece of money
12. Up to this time or place
13. Kind regard
14. The face
18. Young of an animal
21. Gain in any desirable thing
24. To strike suddenly or violently

Down
1. Understand
3. Very forceful
5. Rude or surly
10. Bed
11. On a journey
15. Wonder
16. Gladly
17. To plan or fabricate
19. Explanation
20. Totally, entirely
22. Trough beneath a grape press
23. Any person without exception

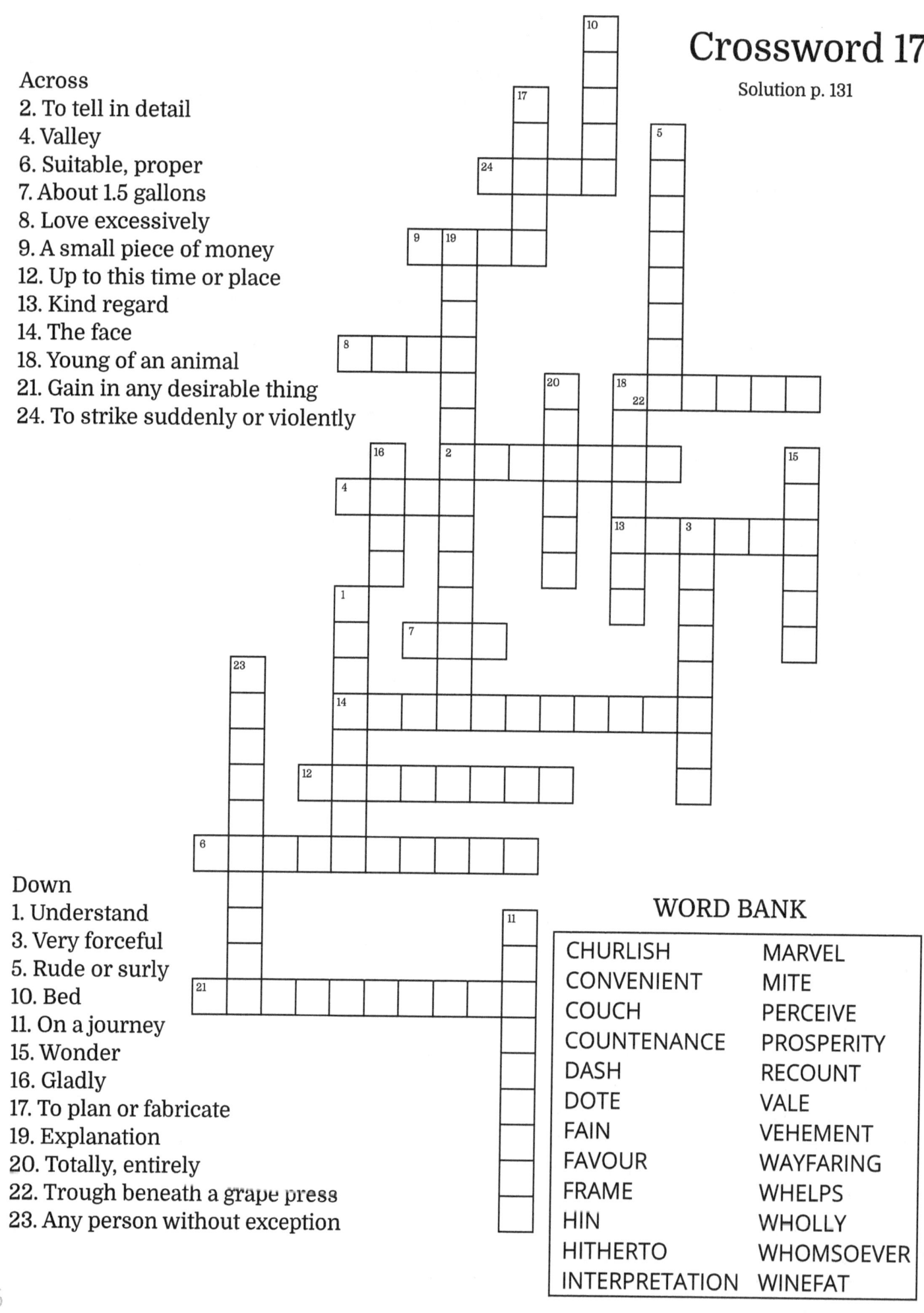

WORD BANK

CHURLISH	MARVEL
CONVENIENT	MITE
COUCH	PERCEIVE
COUNTENANCE	PROSPERITY
DASH	RECOUNT
DOTE	VALE
FAIN	VEHEMENT
FAVOUR	WAYFARING
FRAME	WHELPS
HIN	WHOLLY
HITHERTO	WHOMSOEVER
INTERPRETATION	WINEFAT

Pinwheels #3

Solution p. 119

The answer to each numbered clue will either begin or end with the letter in the center of each pinwheel. Write a word from inside to outside or outside to inside as needed.

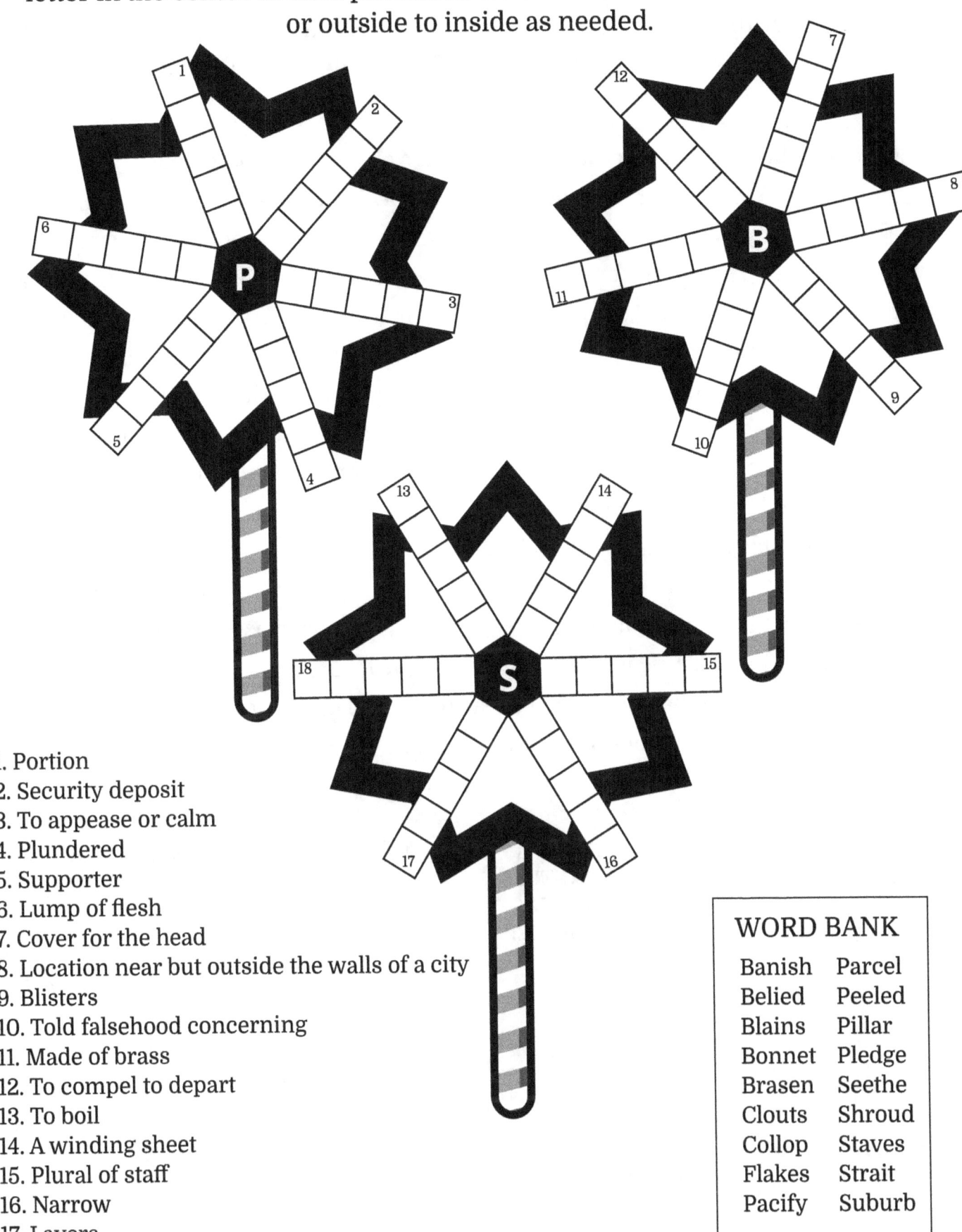

1. Portion
2. Security deposit
3. To appease or calm
4. Plundered
5. Supporter
6. Lump of flesh
7. Cover for the head
8. Location near but outside the walls of a city
9. Blisters
10. Told falsehood concerning
11. Made of brass
12. To compel to depart
13. To boil
14. A winding sheet
15. Plural of staff
16. Narrow
17. Layers
18. Patched clothes

WORD BANK

Banish	Parcel
Belied	Peeled
Blains	Pillar
Bonnet	Pledge
Brasen	Seethe
Clouts	Shroud
Collop	Staves
Flakes	Strait
Pacify	Suburb

Fill in the Blank - Isaiah Chapter 3

Use the definitions in parentheses to select the words that belong in the text and write them in the blanks. Check your answers in your Bible.

[16] Moreover the Lord saith, Because the daughters of Zion are (proud and disdainful) _____, and walk with stretched forth necks and (ogling) _____ eyes, walking and (putting on airs) _____ as they go, and making a tinkling with their feet: [17] Therefore the Lord will smite with a scab the crown of the head of the daughters of Zion, and the Lord will discover their secret parts. [18] In that day the Lord will take away the (showy appearance) _____ of their tinkling ornaments about their feet, and their (hairnets) _____, and their round (headdresses) _____ like the moon, [19] The chains, and the bracelets, and the (face coverings) _____, [20] The bonnets, and the ornaments of the legs, and the headbands, and the tablets, and the earrings, [21] The rings, and nose jewels, [22] The changeable suits of apparel, and the (cloaks) _____, and the (hoods) _____, and the (curling irons) _____, [23] The glasses, and the fine linen, and the hoods, and the vails. [24] And it shall come to pass, that instead of sweet smell there shall be stink; and instead of a (belt) _____ a rent; and instead of well set hair baldness; and instead of a (chest ornament) _____ a girding of sackcloth; and burning instead of beauty.

BRAVERY

CAULS

CRISPING PINS

GIRDLE

HAUGHTY

MANTLES

MINCING

MUFFLERS

STOMACHER

TIRES

WANTON

WIMPLES

Compound Words #3

Match the two parts of each compound word using the definition. Write the letter of the second half in the blank space following the first half.   Solution p. 123

1. Common saying =	BY	+ _____	A. BEARER
2. Curling iron =	CRISPING	+ _____	B. COURSE
3. Attendant who conveys drinks =	CUP	+ _____	C. FOLD
4. Without wetting the feet =	DRY	+ _____	D. FRUITS
5. Dish used to hold or move fire =	FIRE	+ _____	E. HEARTED
6. Produce first matured and collected =	FIRST	+ _____	F. HOOK
7. Infantry soldiers =	FOOT	+ _____	G. KNIFE
8. Front =	FORE	+ _____	H. MAN
9. A messenger sent before =	FORE	+ _____	I. MAN
10. Husband =	GOOD	+ _____	J. MARK
11. Javelins =	HAND	+ _____	K. MASTER
12. The last =	HINDER	+ _____	L. MEDDLE
13. To interfere in the affairs of others =	INTER	+ _____	M. MEN
14. A male of the same family =	KINS	+ _____	N. MOST
15. Joyful =	MERRY	+ _____	O. NECKED
16. Rejected matter =	OFF	+ _____	P. NIGHT
17. To catch =	OVER	+ _____	Q. OUT
18. To be crushed beneath =	OVER	+ _____	R. PAN
19. Small blade for carving =	PEN	+ _____	S. PART
20. Instrument used to shape trees =	PRUNING	+ _____	T. PIN
21. Identical =	SELF	+ _____	U. ROBE
22. Place where sheep are confined =	SHEEP	+ _____	V. RUNNER
23. Stubborn =	STIFF	+ _____	W. SAME
24. One who burdens with labor =	TASK	+ _____	X. SCOURING
25. Support =	UNDER	+ _____	Y. SETTER
26. Place where clothing is kept =	WARD	+ _____	Z. SHOD
27. A stream or brook =	WATER	+ _____	AA. STAVES
28. Guidepost =	WAY	+ _____	BB. TAKE
29. Outside =	WITH	+ _____	CC. WHELM
30. The previous evening =	YESTER	+ _____	DD. WORD

Crossword 18

Solution p. 131

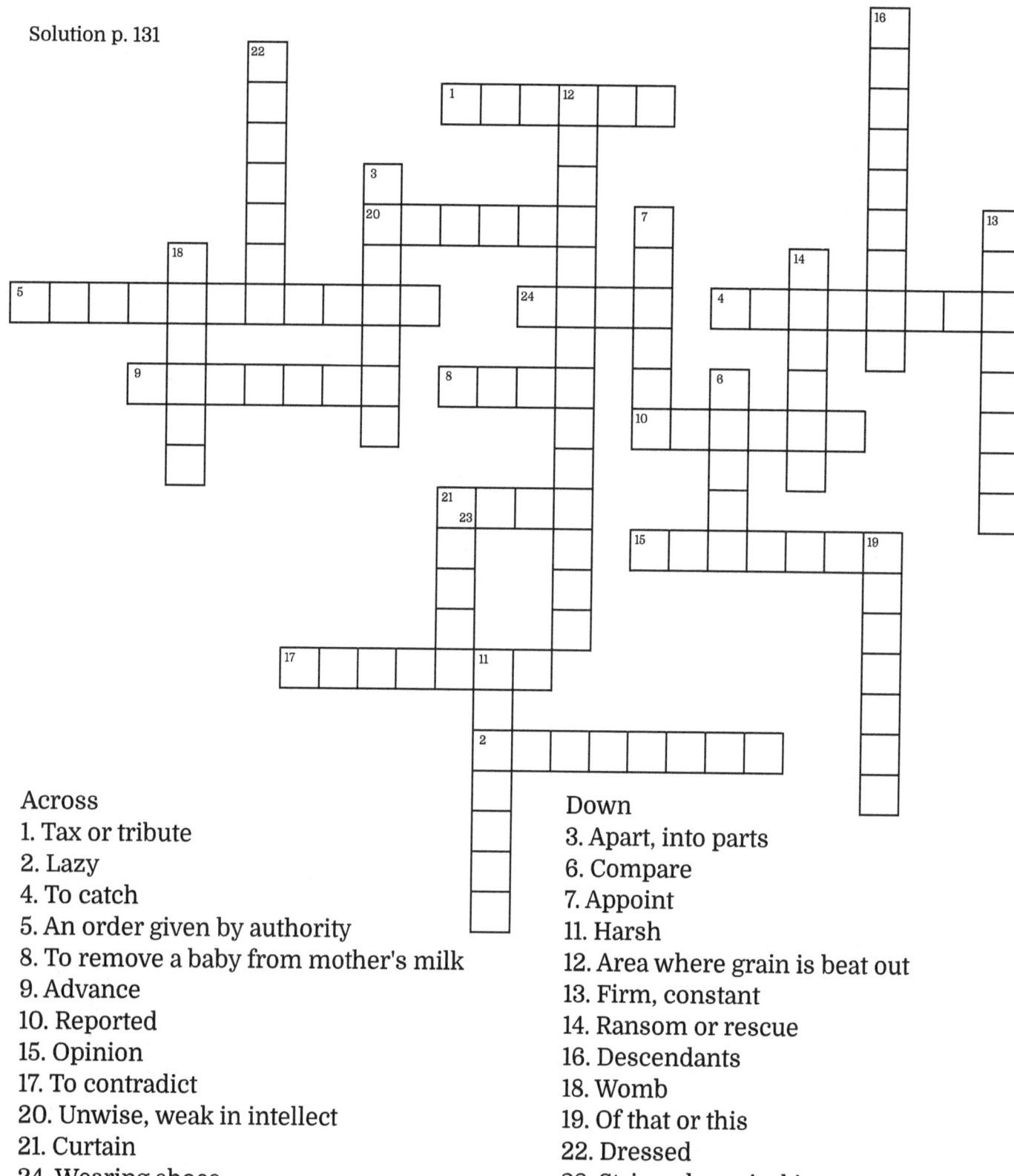

Across
1. Tax or tribute
2. Lazy
4. To catch
5. An order given by authority
8. To remove a baby from mother's milk
9. Advance
10. Reported
15. Opinion
17. To contradict
20. Unwise, weak in intellect
21. Curtain
24. Wearing shoes

Down
3. Apart, into parts
6. Compare
7. Appoint
11. Harsh
12. Area where grain is beat out
13. Firm, constant
14. Ransom or rescue
16. Descendants
18. Womb
19. Of that or this
22. Dressed
23. Stringed musical instruments

WORD BANK			
ARRAYED	GAINSAY	POSTERITY	STEDFAST
ASUNDER	LIKEN	PROMOTE	THEREOF
AUSTERE	MATRIX	REDEEM	THRESHINGFLOOR
COMMANDMENT	NOISED	SHOD	VAIL
CONCEIT	ORDAIN	SIMPLE	VIOLS
CUSTOM	OVERTAKE	SLOTHFUL	WEAN

One of Each

Solution p. 123

Select one letter from each column (in order from one to six) and write the answer to each numbered clue. Use the Scripture reference if you need help.

	1	2	3	4	5	6
1.	hfp	emi	rnb	tar	dlr	abd
2.	wmo	obh	seu	fmv	tui	lvn
3.	jya	wxu	dsm	jxt	lko	fme
4.	dcv	wut	jxr	dwf	zlb	ose
5.	yrs	smt	scr	wih	vsl	aer
6.	fce	ros	svy	xfe	ern	otw
7.	rdm	eda	tgu	mai	grj	eln
8.	fws	mla	wab	ugc	vot	nko
9.	ihc	goe	rbe	nwp	edo	uct
10.	zdr	ebl	gbp	woy	ksh	lef
11.	cay	fow	tbu	rbv	wsd	ebc
12.	gmq	wur	dea	zuv	fer	hln
13.	snv	lco	ucs	rpt	cvn	nyd

1. Proclaimer (Dan. 3:4) _____

2. Filled with distress or sorrow (Jer. 17:16) _____

3. To run into or clash against (Nahum 2:4) _____

4. To thicken or clot (Job 10:10) _____

5. To put forth effort, to contend (Gen. 26:20) _____

6. Shelter (Is. 4:6) _____

7. Withdraw (2 Sam. 11:15) _____

8. Narrow mouthed vessel for liquids (1 Chron. 16:3) _____

9. Wind instrument of music (Dan. 3:15) _____

10. To remove from office (Dan. 5:20) _____

11. Work shift (Luke 1:8) _____

12. Carved or sculpted (Ex. 20:4) _____

13. Having diseased skin (Lev. 22:22) _____

Snowflakes #6

Solution p. 123

Select a word from the word bank for each numbered clue and write it across the snowflake. When you have filled in all the answers, some of the letters on the edges will spell a word from the Bible. Write each letter on its corresponding number to reveal the word.

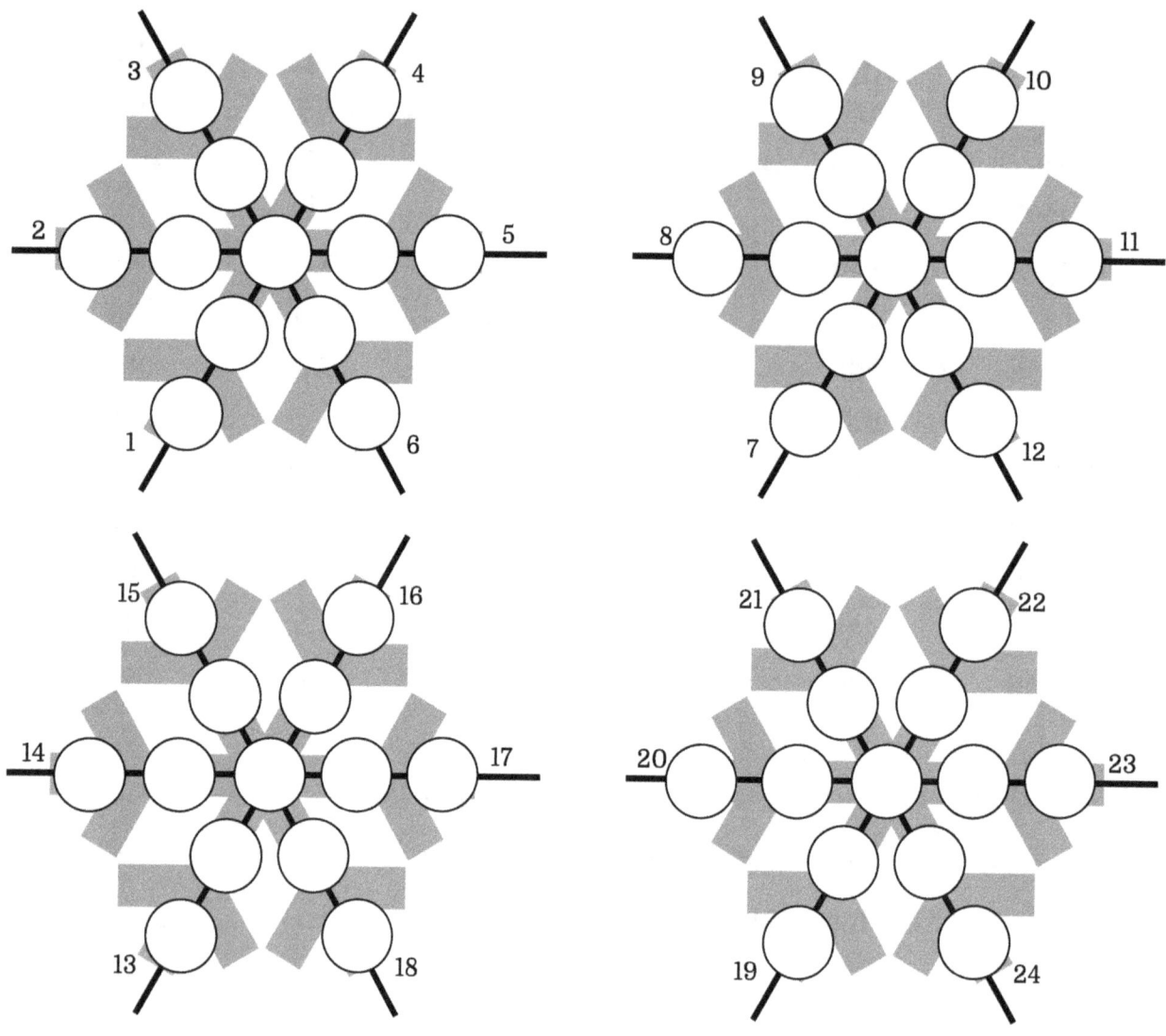

1. An enclosed part of the entrance into a place
2. A place frequently visited
3. Report
7. Paralysis
8. Lack of understanding
9. Lentils, peas, or beans

13. Untamed
14. To cause to make a noise
15. To hold without right
19. Cover
20. Frolick
21. Anything troublesome

Word Bank

BRUIT	CLOKE	FOLLY	PALSY	SOUND	THORN
BRUTE	COURT	HAUNT	PULSE	SPORT	USURP

8-Letter word from Jude 1:15 _ _ _ _ _ _ _ _
                              20 7 12 22 1 2 16 14

Anagrams #6

Each word set is an anagram of a single Bible word. Use the definition to unscramble them. Stumped? Use the reference verse for help.   Solution p. 125

Example: Owing something to someone   bend diet   __indebted__

1. Affirmed (Deuteronomy 26:17)   havoc due   _ _ _ _ _ _ _ _ _
2. Procreated (John 3:16)   ten to beg   _ _ _ _ _ _ _ _ _
3. Betrothings (Song of Solomon 3:11)   soup sales   _ _ _ _ _ _ _ _ _
4. Demonic (Leviticus 20:27)   if I alarm   _ _ _ _ _ _ _ _ _
5. Feeble or disabled (John 5:3)   tip me not   _ _ _ _ _ _ _ _ _
6. Made light by fermentation (Exodus 12:34)   even deal   _ _ _ _ _ _ _ _ _
7. Apparent; obvious (Ephesians 5:13)   safe mint   _ _ _ _ _ _ _ _ _
8. To dwell on in thought (Psalm 143:5)   diet team   _ _ _ _ _ _ _ _ _
9. Devouring (Matthew 7:15)   grave inn   _ _ _ _ _ _ _ _ _
10. Angels (Isaiah 6:2)   marsh pies   _ _ _ _ _ _ _ _ _
11. Inform (Ruth 4:4)   drive seat   _ _ _ _ _ _ _ _ _
12. Bows and arrows (1 Samuel 20:40)   trial rely   _ _ _ _ _ _ _ _ _
13. Adorned with needlework (Ezekiel 16:13)   bored ride   _ _ _ _ _ _ _ _ _
14. Withdrawn (Job 19:13)   garden set   _ _ _ _ _ _ _ _ _
15. That cannot be healed (2 Chronicles 21:18)   brain clue   _ _ _ _ _ _ _ _ _
16. Stubborn (Isaiah 48:4)   saint to be   _ _ _ _ _ _ _ _ _
17. Put in danger (Judges 5:18)   jaded rope   _ _ _ _ _ _ _ _ _
18. Compelled (Luke 24:29)   consider ant   _ _ _ _ _ _ _ _ _
19. Uniting metallic substances (Isaiah 41:7)   rinse dog   _ _ _ _ _ _ _ _ _
20. Lazy (Proverbs 12:27)   full shot   _ _ _ _ _ _ _ _ _
21. Caution (2 Chronicles 2:12)   crude pen   _ _ _ _ _ _ _ _ _
22. Particular (1 Peter 2:9)   clue pair   _ _ _ _ _ _ _ _ _
23. Supply (Ephesians 4:29)   stir mine   _ _ _ _ _ _ _ _ _

Finish the Word #7

All of these nouns have the same ending. Can you finish them, using the definitions and word list?
The number of blanks indicates the number of missing letters.

Definition	Answer	Word List
Emptiness	_ _ _ ITY	ADVERSITY
Justice, right	_ _ _ ITY	AFFINITY
Truth	_ _ _ ITY	ANTIQUITY
Ill will	_ _ _ ITY	CAPTIVITY
Time, manner, and place of birth	_ _ _ _ _ _ ITY	ENMITY
Sin, wickedness	_ _ _ _ _ _ ITY	EQUITY
Faithfulness	_ _ _ _ _ _ ITY	FIDELITY
Lowliness of mind	_ _ _ _ _ _ ITY	HOSPITALITY
Relation by marriage	_ _ _ _ _ _ ITY	HUMILITY
Darkness	_ _ _ _ _ _ _ ITY	IMPORTUNITY
Religious ceremony	_ _ _ _ _ _ _ ITY	INFIRMITY
Great age	_ _ _ _ _ _ _ ITY	INIQUITY
Descendants	_ _ _ _ _ _ _ ITY	INTEGRITY
Subjection	_ _ _ _ _ _ _ ITY	MALIGNITY
Weakness	_ _ _ _ _ _ _ ITY	NATIVITY
Evil disposition towards another	_ _ _ _ _ _ _ ITY	NECESSITY
That which must be	_ _ _ _ _ _ _ ITY	OBSCURITY
Misfortune	_ _ _ _ _ _ _ ITY	PARTIALITY
Uprightness in moral character	_ _ _ _ _ _ _ ITY	PERPLEXITY
Maidenhood	_ _ _ _ _ _ _ ITY	POSTERITY
Astonishment	_ _ _ _ _ _ _ _ ITY	PROSPERITY
Gain in any desirable thing	_ _ _ _ _ _ _ _ ITY	SIMPLICITY
Bias of judgment	_ _ _ _ _ _ _ _ ITY	SOLEMNITY
Sincerity	_ _ _ _ _ _ _ _ ITY	SUPERFLUITY
Abundance	_ _ _ _ _ _ _ _ ITY	VANITY
Persistent request	_ _ _ _ _ _ _ _ _ ITY	VERITY
Entertaining guests	_ _ _ _ _ _ _ _ _ ITY	VIRGINITY

Solution p. 120

Select-A-Syllable #6

Each of the answers to the following clues is made up of two syllables that can be found in the box. Put them together and write your completed words in the spaces provided. The numbers in parentheses indicate the total number of letters in each answer. Each syllable will be used only once.   Solution p. 121

1. To draw (8)   _____

2. Accommodate (7)   _____

3. To bear or support (7)   _____

4. Captive held in order to secure certain conditions (7)   _____

5. Loaded (5)   _____

6. To make or form anything (7)   _____

7. Majestic (7)   _____

8. A section of a place (7)   _____

9. Adorn (7)   _____

10. To sign one's name to (9)   _____

11. Attempt to overthrow the government (7)   _____

12. A deep, dark prison (7)   _____

13. Family room (7)   _____

14. To give a tendency (7)   _____

15. Increase (7)   _____

16. Hard, brittle cake (8)   _____

17. A little drum (7)   _____

18. Adolescent male (9)   _____

19. To include (8)   _____

20. Dead body (7)   _____

Syllable Box

AUG	CRACK	IN	NISH	STRIP
BE	DUN	ION	PAR	SUB
BREL	EN	LAD	POUR	SUS
CAR	ER	LING	QUART	TAGE
CASE	FASH	LOUR	SCRIBE	TAIN
CLINE	GAR	LY	SON	TIM
CLUDE	GEON	MENT	STATE	TRAY
CON	HOS	NEL	STEAD	TREA

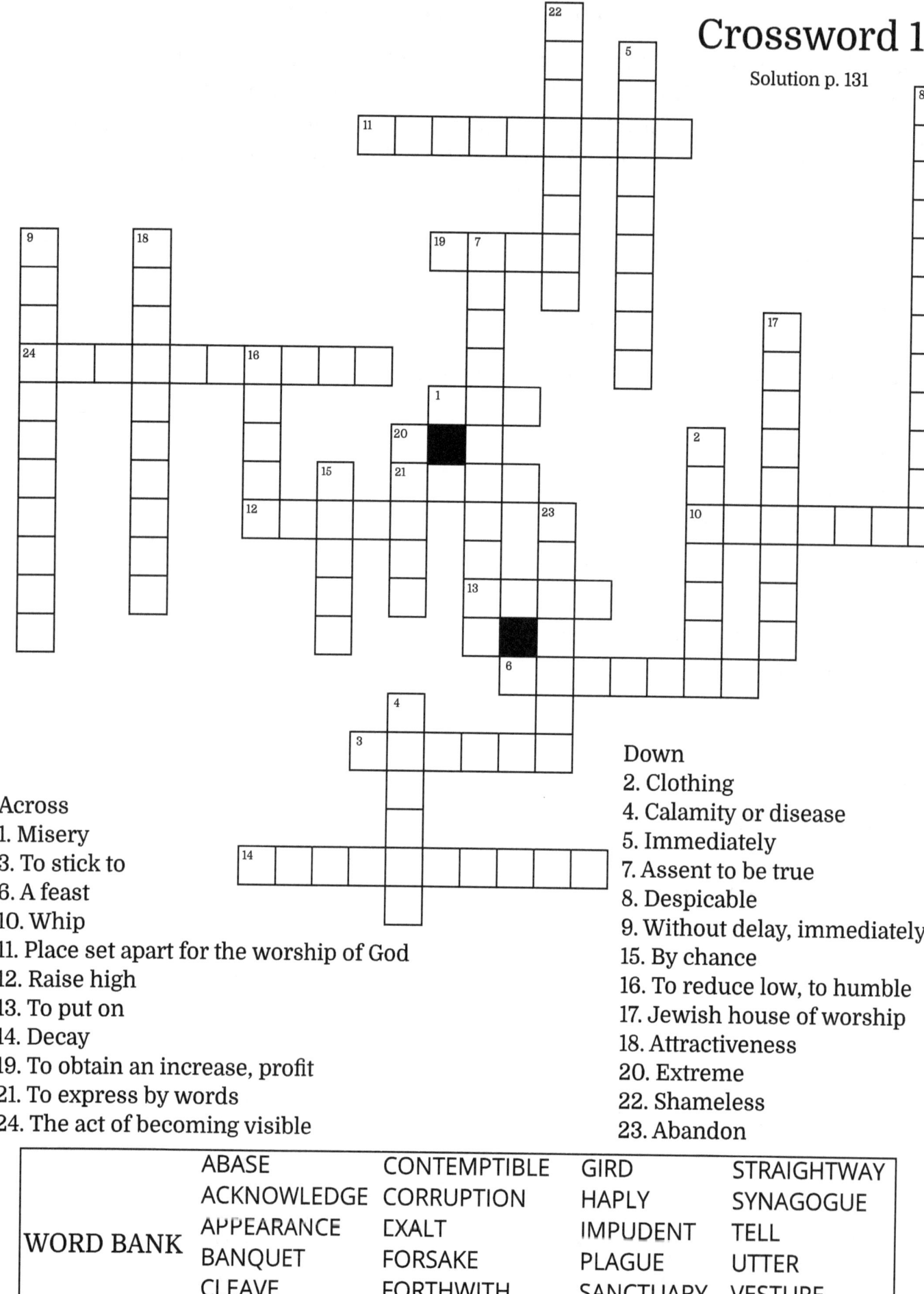

Crossword 19

Solution p. 131

Across

1. Misery
3. To stick to
6. A feast
10. Whip
11. Place set apart for the worship of God
12. Raise high
13. To put on
14. Decay
19. To obtain an increase, profit
21. To express by words
24. The act of becoming visible

Down

2. Clothing
4. Calamity or disease
5. Immediately
7. Assent to be true
8. Despicable
9. Without delay, immediately
15. By chance
16. To reduce low, to humble
17. Jewish house of worship
18. Attractiveness
20. Extreme
22. Shameless
23. Abandon

WORD BANK			
ABASE	CONTEMPTIBLE	GIRD	STRAIGHTWAY
ACKNOWLEDGE	CORRUPTION	HAPLY	SYNAGOGUE
APPEARANCE	EXALT	IMPUDENT	TELL
BANQUET	FORSAKE	PLAGUE	UTTER
CLEAVE	FORTHWITH	SANCTUARY	VESTURE
COMELINESS	GAIN	SCOURGE	WOE

Word Search

Find today's version of each archaic word in the word search.
Write it in the blank. Solution p. 122

P	H	L	Y	L	E	U	W	N	L	L	K	Y	J	M
Q	L	U	Z	U	O	Q	O	H	W	N	T	Y	M	R
Z	E	A	Z	K	Y	R	W	U	N	F	J	U	L	U
A	D	H	J	S	M	G	Y	P	S	T	L	E	E	Y
P	S	J	M	R	B	Y	A	R	T	E	B	N	N	D
K	P	T	T	Y	V	K	R	P	R	D	G	W	O	C
J	D	R	O	W	V	B	T	R	E	R	E	I	M	O
U	F	E	U	N	C	C	X	I	A	G	R	D	S	P
Y	E	A	L	J	I	J	H	V	K	C	L	O	H	E
J	D	T	G	T	D	S	E	A	D	K	T	A	L	E
L	O	B	O	D	O	E	H	T	M	Q	Q	O	R	L
Y	R	P	E	L	E	I	P	E	U	P	A	B	B	Y
L	M	I	I	Y	A	R	N	L	D	D	A	L	B	O
K	M	A	R	S	H	Z	A	Y	E	Y	I	I	V	E
K	L	X	Q	X	S	L	S	D	B	H	M	B	N	O

ASTONIED _ _ _ _ _ _ _ _ _ _ _ _ _ _ _ _

BADE _ _ _ _ _ _ _ _ _ _ _ _ _ _ _ _

BEWRAY _ _ _ _ _ _ _ _ _ _ _ _ _ _ _ _

CHAMPAIGN _ _ _ _ _ _ _ _ _ _ _ _ _ _ _ _

DURST _ _ _ _ _ _ _ _ _ _ _ _ _ _ _ _

ENTREAT _ _ _ _ _ _ _ _ _ _ _ _ _ _ _ _

GRAVE _ _ _ _ _ _ _ _ _ _ _ _ _ _ _ _

HALE

HOLPEN _ _ _ _ _ _ _ _ _ _ _ _ _ _ _ _

LADEN _ _ _ _ _ _ _ _ _ _ _ _ _ _ _ _

MARISH _ _ _ _ _ _ _ _ _ _ _ _ _ _ _ _

PILL _ _ _ _ _ _ _ _ _ _ _ _ _ _ _ _

PRIVILY _ _ _ _ _ _ _ _ _ _ _ _ _ _ _ _

RIE _ _ _ _ _ _ _ _ _ _ _ _ _ _ _ _

STRAKE _ _ _ _ _ _ _ _ _ _ _ _ _ _ _ _

SUP _ _ _ _ _ _ _ _ _ _ _ _ _ _ _ _

107

Down the Stairs #5

Use the definitions to place words from the word bank into each row. One letter is given in each word.

Solution p. 122

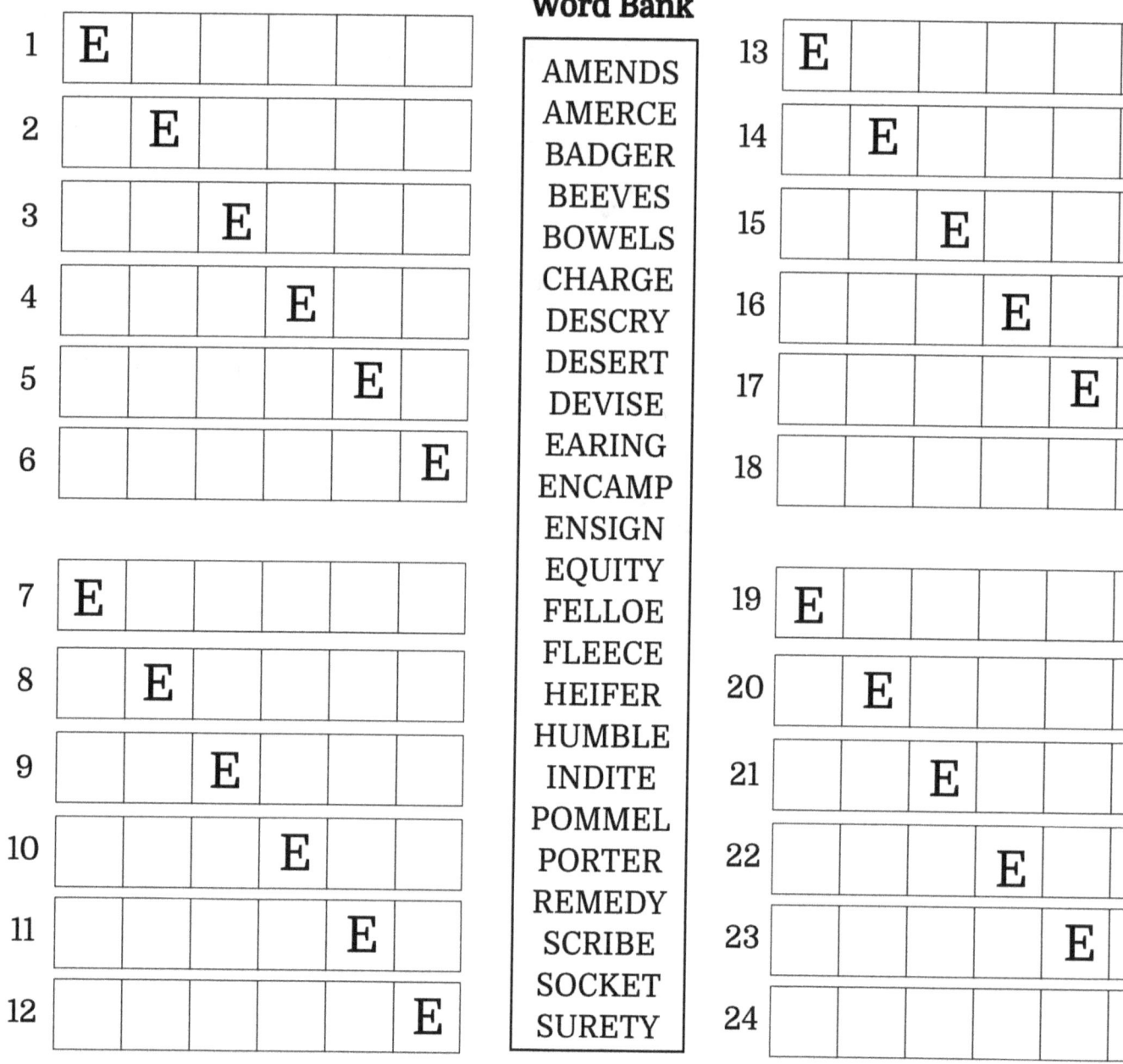

Word Bank

AMENDS
AMERCE
BADGER
BEEVES
BOWELS
CHARGE
DESCRY
DESERT
DEVISE
EARING
ENCAMP
ENSIGN
EQUITY
FELLOE
FLEECE
HEIFER
HUMBLE
INDITE
POMMEL
PORTER
REMEDY
SCRIBE
SOCKET
SURETY

1. Justice, right
2. Explore
3. Compensation
4. Center of human kindness
5. Animal whose skin was used on the tabernacle
6. To dictate what is to be written or spoken
7. To pitch tents
8. Exterior part of a wheel that is supported by spokes
9. Coat of wool from a sheep
10. Reward or punishment merited
11. Hollow piece that holds something else
12. One who reads and explains the law

13. A signal to assemble or notify
14. Invent
15. Inflict a penalty
16. Certainty
17. Keeper of a door or gate
18. Imputation, in a bad sense
19. Plowing
20. A young cow
21. Cattle
22. Cure
23. Something thick or bulky
24. Reduce to a low state

Fill in the Blank - Colossians Chapter 1

Use the definitions in parentheses to select the words that belong in the text and write them in the blanks. Check your answers in your Bible.

9 For this cause we also, since the day we heard it, do not cease to pray for you, and to desire that ye might be filled with the knowledge of his will in all wisdom and spiritual understanding; 10 That ye might walk worthy of the Lord unto all pleasing, being fruitful in every good work, and increasing in the knowledge of God; 11 Strengthened with all might, according to his (excellent) _____ power, unto all patience and (patient) _____ with joyfulness; 12 Giving thanks unto the Father, which hath made us (suitable) _____to be (sharers) _____ of the (estate passed on to descendants) _____ of the saints in light: 13 Who hath delivered us from the power of darkness, and hath (transported) _____ us into the kingdom of his dear Son: 14 In whom we have (deliverance) _____through his blood, even the (pardon) _____ of sins: 15 Who is the image of the (cannot be seen) _____ God, the firstborn of every creature: 16 For by him were all things created, that are in heaven, and that are in earth, visible and invisible, whether they be thrones, or (supreme authorities) _____, or (sovereigns) _____, or powers: all things were created by him, and for him: 17 And he is before all things, and by him all things (stand together) _____. 18 And he is the head of the body, the church: who is the beginning, the firstborn from the dead; that in all things he might have the (priority of place) _____. 19 For it pleased the Father that in him should all (completeness) _____dwell; 20 And, having made peace through the blood of his cross, by him to (restore to union) _____ all things unto himself; by him, I say, whether they be things in earth, or things in heaven.

CONSIST
DOMINIONS
FORGIVENESS
FULNESS
GLORIOUS

INHERITANCE
INVISIBLE
LONGSUFFERING
MEET
PARTAKERS

PREEMINENCE
PRINCIPALITIES
RECONCILE
REDEMPTION
TRANSLATED

Decryption

Solution p. 119

Work back and forth between the definitions and the verse above, transferring letters to the numbered spaces. Some letters will be used more than once.

$\overline{1}\,\overline{63}\,\overline{30}$ $\overline{26}\,\overline{32}\,\overline{8}$ $\overline{13}\,\overline{4}\,\overline{66}\,\overline{2}$ $\overline{39}\,\overline{58}\,\overline{27}\,\overline{20}$ $\overline{24}\,\overline{16}\,\overline{7}\,\overline{18}$ $\overline{57}\,\overline{45}\,\overline{40}\,\overline{17}\,\overline{29}\,\overline{10}'$

$\overline{50}\,\overline{21}\,\overline{67}'$ $\overline{36}$ $\overline{64}\,\overline{34}\,\overline{11}\,\overline{65}$ $\overline{49}\,\overline{62}\,\overline{59}\,\overline{31}\,\overline{37}$ $\overline{51}\,\overline{48}\,\overline{68}\,\overline{4}$ $\overline{28}\,\overline{32}\,\overline{47}\,\overline{53}\,\overline{42}$ $\overline{17}\,\overline{6}\,\overline{46}\,\overline{2}$

#3 J E R I C H O,
$\overline{57}\,\overline{38}\,\overline{41}\,\overline{54}\,\overline{5}\,\overline{32}\,\overline{15}$ $\overline{34}\,\overline{48}\,\overline{30}$ $\overline{26}\,\overline{17}\,\overline{60}$ $\overline{44}\,\overline{12}\,\overline{22}\,\overline{52}$ $\overline{7}\,\overline{64}\,\overline{65}\,\overline{41}\,\overline{33}\,\overline{4}\,\overline{55}'$ $\overline{58}\,\overline{16}\,\overline{20}$

$\overline{28}\,\overline{64}\,\overline{42}$ $\overline{23}\,\overline{69}\,\overline{49}\,\overline{32}\,\overline{68}\,\overline{56}$ $\overline{23}\,\overline{8}\,\overline{63}$ $\overline{4}\,\overline{55}$ $\overline{3}\,\overline{10}\,\overline{25}\,\overline{18}\,\overline{24}\,\overline{66}.$

1. One who pleads for another
        V
$\overline{1}\,\overline{2}\,\overline{3}\,\overline{4}\,\overline{5}\,\overline{6}\,\overline{7}\,\overline{8}$

2. A covering
P
$\overline{9}\,\overline{10}\,\overline{11}\,\overline{12}\,\overline{13}\,\overline{14}\,\overline{15}\,\overline{16}$

3. Held
    D
$\overline{17}\,\overline{18}\,\overline{19}\,\overline{20}\,\overline{21}\,\overline{22}$

4. A great number; a crowd
U
$\overline{23}\,\overline{24}\,\overline{25}\,\overline{26}\,\overline{27}\,\overline{28}\,\overline{29}\,\overline{30}\,\overline{31}$

5. Depression of spirit
     N
$\overline{32}\,\overline{33}\,\overline{34}\,\overline{35}\,\overline{36}\,\overline{37}\,\overline{38}\,\overline{39}\,\overline{40}$

6. Account taken
   K
$\overline{41}\,\overline{42}\,\overline{43}\,\overline{44}\,\overline{45}\,\overline{46}\,\overline{47}\,\overline{48}\,\overline{49}$

7. To communicate by sign or word
      Y
$\overline{50}\,\overline{51}\,\overline{52}\,\overline{53}\,\overline{54}\,\overline{55}\,\overline{56}$

8. A long spear
   L
$\overline{57}\,\overline{58}\,\overline{59}\,\overline{60}\,\overline{61}\,\overline{62}\,\overline{63}$

9. Person who holds doctrines contrary to Scripture
   T
$\overline{64}\,\overline{65}\,\overline{66}\,\overline{67}\,\overline{68}\,\overline{69}\,\overline{70}\,\overline{71}$

$\overline{5}\,\overline{75}\,\overline{20}\,\overline{16}\,\overline{44}$ $\overline{31}\,\overline{18}\,\overline{22}$ $\overline{68}\,\overline{72}\,\overline{47}\,\overline{21}\,\overline{7}$ $\overline{6}\,\overline{46}\,\overline{50}\,\overline{60}\,\overline{28}\,\overline{40}\,\overline{69}\,\overline{52}$ $\overline{9}\,\overline{27}\,\overline{55}$ $\overline{13}$

$\overline{80}\,\overline{23}\,\overline{54}\,\overline{36}\,\overline{72}\,\overline{48}\,\overline{3}\,\overline{24}$ $\overline{10}\,\overline{57}$ $\overline{1}\,\overline{4}\,\overline{19}\,\overline{34}\,\overline{23}\,\overline{35}$: $\overline{57}\,\overline{62}\,\overline{2}$ $\overline{70}\,\overline{65}\,\overline{44}$ $\overline{75}\,\overline{9}$ $\overline{44}\,\overline{6}\,\overline{51}$

#4
$\overline{46}\,\overline{1}\,\overline{20}\,\overline{71}\,\overline{52}\,\overline{30}\,\overline{50}\,\overline{76}\,\overline{49}$ $\overline{18}\,\overline{9}$ $\overline{39}\,\overline{80}$ C O M P L A I N T
$\overline{26}\,\overline{62}\,\overline{66}\,\overline{53}\,\overline{35}\,\overline{30}\,\overline{69}\,\overline{63}\,\overline{68}$ $\overline{13}\,\overline{31}\,\overline{60}$

$\overline{41}\,\overline{77}\,\overline{38}\,\overline{7}\,\overline{57}$ $\overline{6}\,\overline{40}\,\overline{17}\,\overline{15}$ $\overline{58}$ $\overline{8}\,\overline{67}\,\overline{10}\,\overline{14}\,\overline{59}\,\overline{16}$ $\overline{72}\,\overline{56}\,\overline{22}\,\overline{6}\,\overline{42}\,\overline{37}\,\overline{48}\,\overline{27}.$

1. Trousers
    E
$\overline{1}\,\overline{2}\,\overline{3}\,\overline{4}\,\overline{5}\,\overline{6}\,\overline{7}\,\overline{8}$

2. Abandoned
    S
$\overline{9}\,\overline{10}\,\overline{11}\,\overline{12}\,\overline{13}\,\overline{14}\,\overline{15}\,\overline{16}$

3. Proceeding from choice or free will
        Y
$\overline{17}\,\overline{18}\,\overline{19}\,\overline{20}\,\overline{21}\,\overline{22}\,\overline{23}\,\overline{24}\,\overline{25}$

4. Assembly of people
    P
$\overline{26}\,\overline{27}\,\overline{28}\,\overline{29}\,\overline{30}\,\overline{31}\,\overline{32}$

5. A long journey
         G
$\overline{33}\,\overline{34}\,\overline{35}\,\overline{36}\,\overline{37}\,\overline{38}\,\overline{39}\,\overline{40}\,\overline{41}\,\overline{42}$

6. Distressed
   R
$\overline{43}\,\overline{44}\,\overline{45}\,\overline{46}\,\overline{47}\,\overline{48}\,\overline{49}\,\overline{50}\,\overline{51}\,\overline{52}$

7. Free from pollution
    F
$\overline{53}\,\overline{54}\,\overline{55}\,\overline{56}\,\overline{57}\,\overline{58}\,\overline{59}\,\overline{60}$

8. A wasting
    U
$\overline{61}\,\overline{62}\,\overline{63}\,\overline{64}\,\overline{65}\,\overline{66}\,\overline{67}\,\overline{68}\,\overline{69}\,\overline{70}\,\overline{71}$

9. False pretense
H
$\overline{72}\,\overline{73}\,\overline{74}\,\overline{75}\,\overline{76}\,\overline{77}\,\overline{78}\,\overline{79}\,\overline{80}$

Cookie Sheet #5

Use the definitions to unscramble the letters in each cookie. Write your
answers on the dotted lines.

Solution p. 124

Whip

Part

Gray

To ask

To try

Deep

Deliverance

Seriousness

Alienated

Retribution

Aromatic oil

A killing

Carnal

Mildness

Indulgent

Without limits

111

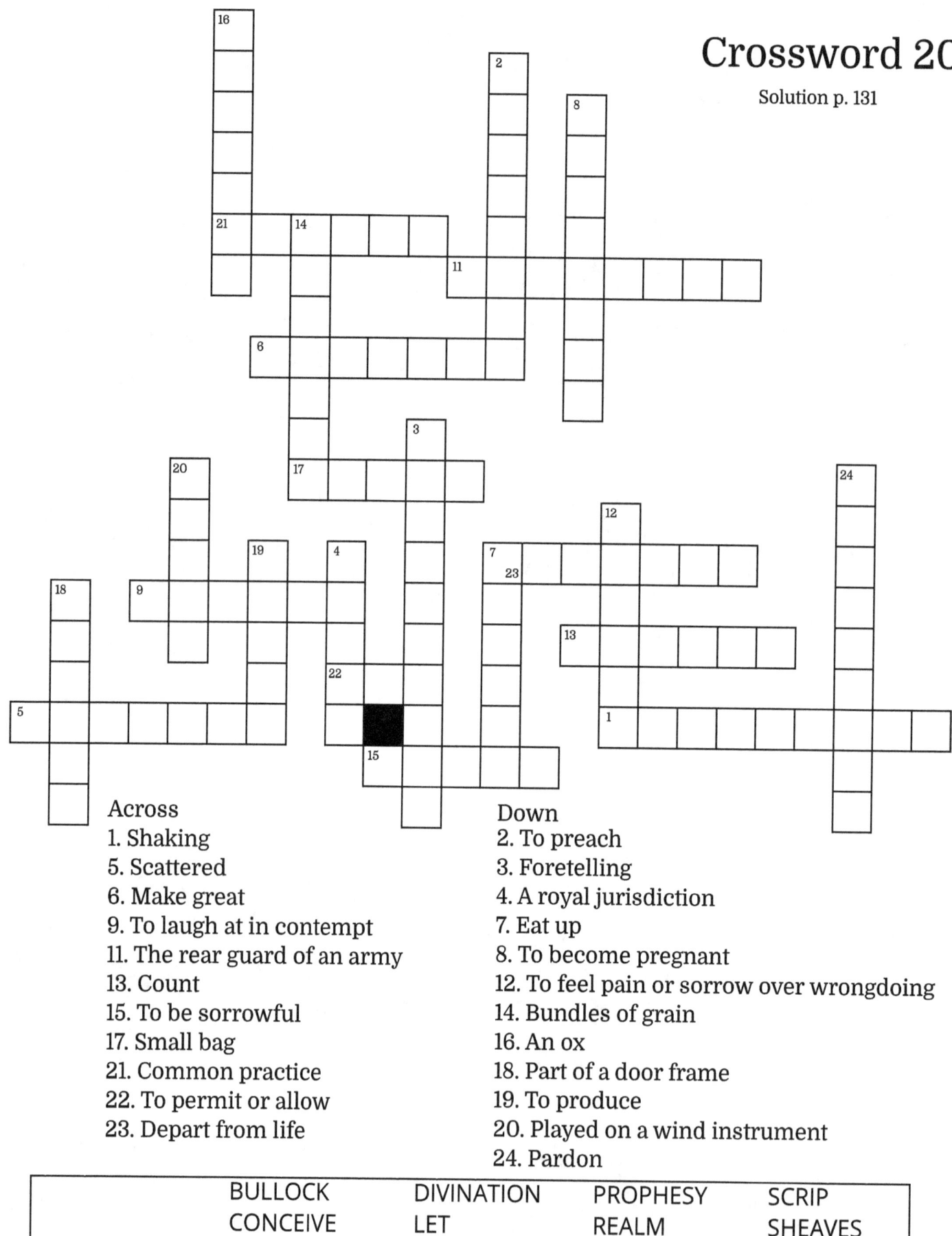

Crossword 20

Solution p. 131

Across

1. Shaking
5. Scattered
6. Make great
9. To laugh at in contempt
11. The rear guard of an army
13. Count
15. To be sorrowful
17. Small bag
21. Common practice
22. To permit or allow
23. Depart from life

Down

2. To preach
3. Foretelling
4. A royal jurisdiction
7. Eat up
8. To become pregnant
12. To feel pain or sorrow over wrongdoing
14. Bundles of grain
16. An ox
18. Part of a door frame
19. To produce
20. Played on a wind instrument
24. Pardon

WORD BANK

BULLOCK	DIVINATION	PROPHESY	SCRIP
CONCEIVE	LET	REALM	SHEAVES
CUSTOM	LINTEL	RECKON	STRAWED
DECEASE	MAGNIFY	REMISSION	TREMBLING
DERIDE	MOURN	REPENT	YIELD
DEVOUR	PIPED	REREWARD	

Common Denominator #3

Each of the answers to the following clues is made up of three segments (NOT syllables). The words have one segment in common which is in its correct position. Choose the others from the box and write them in the spaces provided.

Solution p. 132

	Beginning	Middle	End
1. To give information to	_____	__ER__	_____
2. Reservoir for water	_____	__ER__	_____
3. Predictor of events using supernatural means	_____	_____	__ER__
4. A maxim of wisdom	_____	__ER__	_____
5. A scoffer, a despiser	_____	_____	__ER__
6. Sexual sin outside of marriage	_____	__ER__	_____
7. Cloth to cover the head	_____	__ER__	_____
8. Distorted from right	_____	__ER__	_____
9. Striking lightly and frequently	_____	__ER__	_____
10. Showy appearance	_____	__ER__	_____
11. Men who fill seams to prevent leaking	_____	__ER__	_____
12. To act against with equal force	_____	__ER__	_____
13. Keeping company	_____	__ER__	_____
14. Officer in a royal household	_____	__ER__	_____
15. United in a league	_____	__ER__	_____

SEGMENTS

ADULT	CHAMB	DIV	ORN	SE
ATE	CHIEF	IN	PERV	TAB
B	CIST	ING	PROV	TIFY
BRAV	CONFED	K	S	VAIL
C	CONV	LAIN	SANT	Y
CALK	COUNT	N	SC	Y

Secret Word #6

Place a word from the box below on each line. The circled letters in each puzzle will spell out a secret word also found in the box (and in the Bible).

Division

Smear with soft ointment

Fragrant ointment

To express by words

Secret Word: _____

Collect money for public use

Cover the inside of a roof

Hate for another's success

Forest

Secret Word: _____

Crosswise threads in fabric

Craw of a bird

Abdominal membrane

Body armor

Secret Word: _____

Inclosure for animals

Move one way and the other

Asked

Black & white striped stone

Secret Word: _____

A row

Empty

Cleared of grass

Cut or chiseled

Secret Word: _____

Ridge of earth

To cut off

To open the mouth wide

Top of the head

Secret Word: _____

BADE	CROP	KEPT	OVEN	VOID
BALM	DAUB	KINE	PARE	WALL
BANK	ENVY	LEVY	PATE	WARD
CAUL	FOAM	MAIL	RANK	WAVE
CIEL	GAPE	MOWN	TELL	WOOD
COTE	HEWN	ONYX	VIEW	WOOF

114

Snowflakes #7

Solution p. 123

Select a word from the word bank for each numbered clue and write it across the snowflake. When you have filled in all the answers, some of the letters on the edges will spell a word from the Bible. Write each letter on its corresponding number to reveal the word.

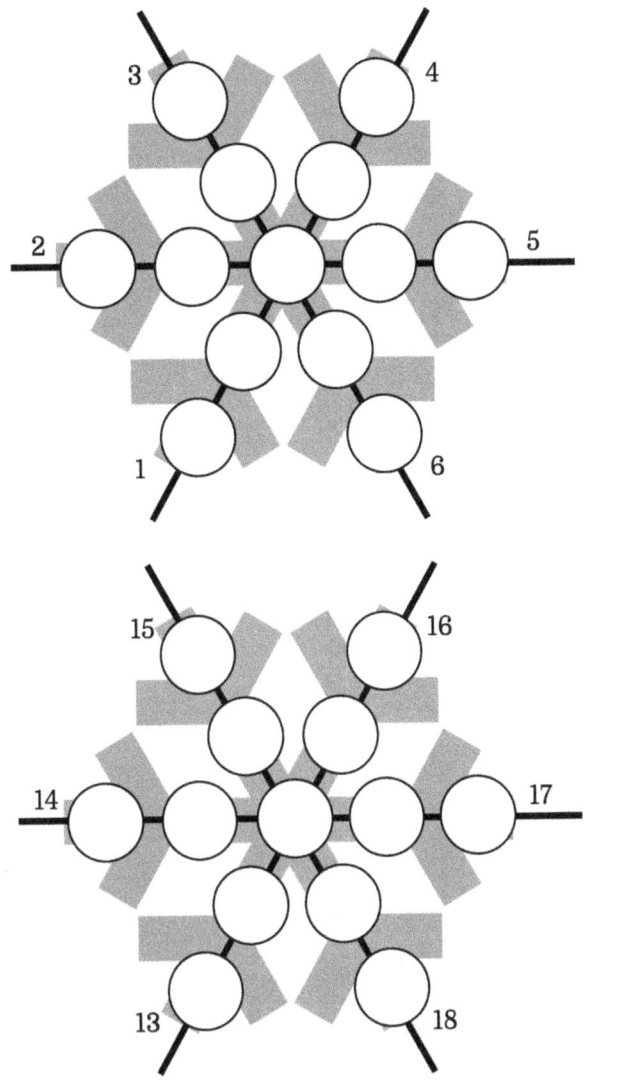

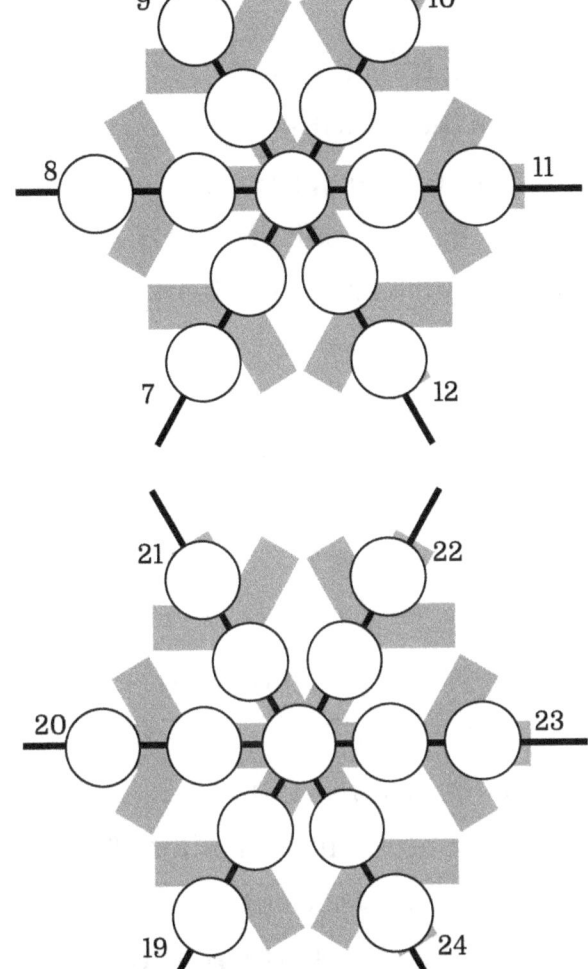

1. Serious
2. Neglectful
3. Entangle
7. Pointed instruments used to make an animal move faster
8. To demand
9. Fret

13. Space
14. Notched end on wood used to fasten it to another piece
15. Young woman of low birth
19. Merry-making
20. Weeds
21. Dared

Word Bank

CHAFE	EXACT	GRAVE	RANGE	SNARE	TENON
DURST	GOADS	MIRTH	SLACK	TARES	WENCH

8-Letter word from Job 1:1 _ _ _ _ _ _ _ _
16 2 9 22 6 15 8 21

Anagrams #7

Each word set is an anagram of a single Bible word. Use the definition to unscramble them. Stumped? Use the reference verse for help.   Solution p. 125

1. Irritation (Psalm 6:1)
2. Rescue (Hebrews 11:35)
3. Not properly mixed (Ezekiel 13:10)
4. That cannot be satisfied (Ezekiel 16:28)
5. Obligation to cover another's debt (Prov. 11:15)
6. Scarcity (Jeremiah 19:9)
7. Dissolving (Isaiah 1:6)
8. Foreign; not native (Nehemiah 13:26)
9. Grand; splendid (1 Chronicles 22:5)
10. Earnest petitions (Proverbs 18:23)
11. Curse (Jeremiah 42:18)
12. To divide by portions (Joshua 13:32)
13. Serpent (Isaiah 14:29)
14. Coat of mail (Jeremiah 46:4)
15. Female who commits adultery (Romans 7:3)
16. Bright red dye (Jeremiah 22:14)
17. Payer to a conquering power (Lamentations 1:1)
18. What is left after removal of a part (Ex. 29:34)
19. Something inherited from ancestors (Deut. 18:8)
20. Capable of being lived in by humans (Prov. 8:31)
21. Descent of a person or family (Ezra 2:62)
22. In pretense (Jeremiah 3:10)

sealed up sir _____

receive land _____

pet under me _____

a snail tube _____

irish setup _____

anti stress _____

tiny fur pig _____

hi adult son _____

failing cam _____

insert a tie _____

torn ice axe _____

sure tidbit _____

artic coke _____

dining bear _____

user salted _____

minor evil _____

rat bury it _____

rider name _____

any import _____

a bible hat _____

go ye glean _____

dingy feel _____

Crossword 21

Solution on p. 132

Down
3. Weeds
5. The most holy place in the temple
6. Suitable
7. That which is inherited
8. Totally
9. Opposition to local civil authority
10. Remarkable
12. To value or esteem
15. Falling from faith into sin
16. Tight clothes
17. Tumor
23. Earnest request, prayer

Across
1. To like
2. To perform one's duties
4. Firmly
11. Tax collector
13. Extravagance
14. That which remains after a part is taken
18. To have as owner
19. Despise or reject
20. Skilled craftsman
21. A thing offered in worship
22. Object form of the second person, personal pronoun, singular
24. Wait

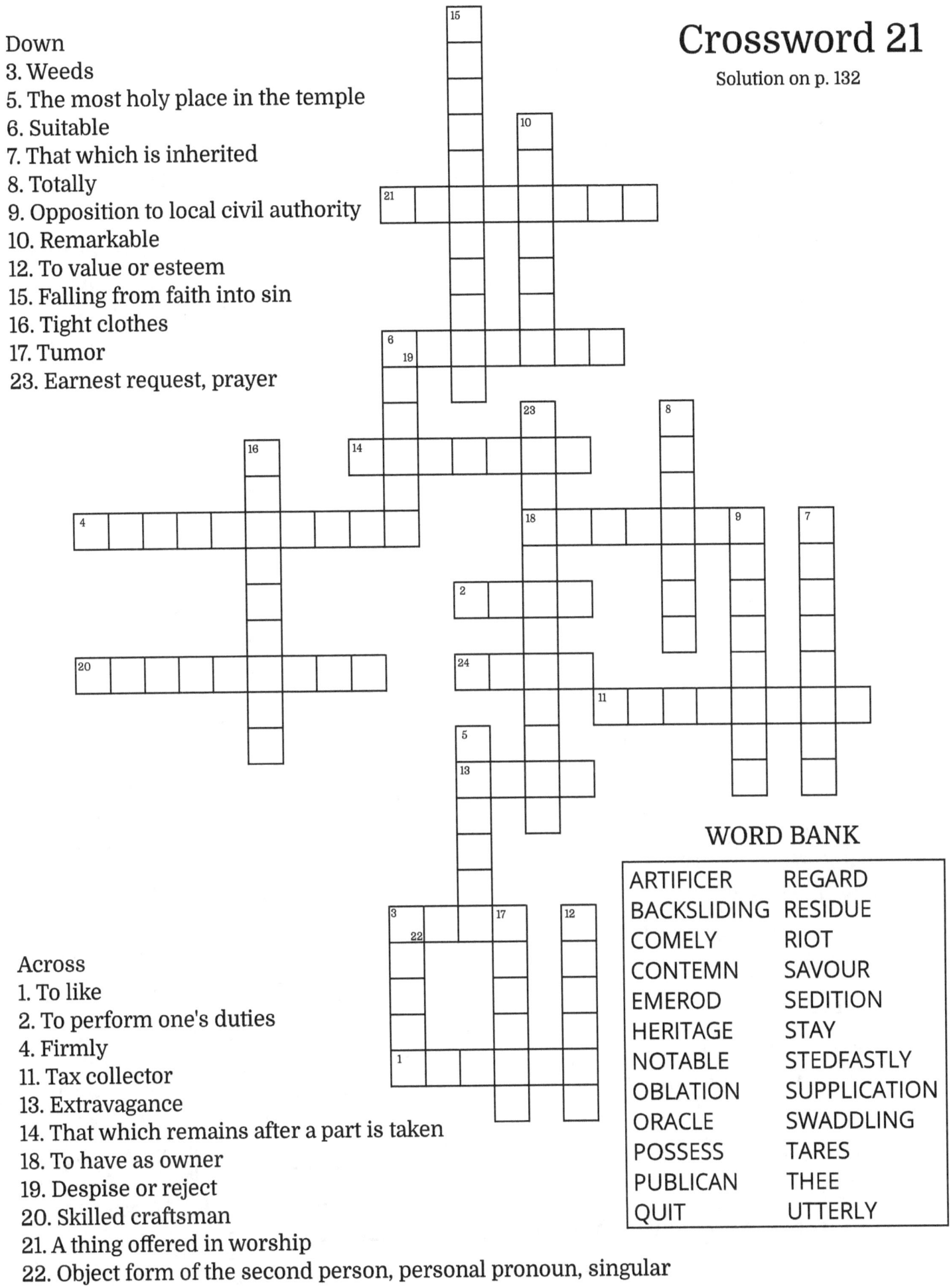

WORD BANK

ARTIFICER	REGARD
BACKSLIDING	RESIDUE
COMELY	RIOT
CONTEMN	SAVOUR
EMEROD	SEDITION
HERITAGE	STAY
NOTABLE	STEDFASTLY
OBLATION	SUPPLICATION
ORACLE	SWADDLING
POSSESS	TARES
PUBLICAN	THEE
QUIT	UTTERLY

Finish the Word #8

All of these adjectives have the same ending. Can you finish them, using the definitions and word list?
The number of blanks indicates the number of missing letters.

Infected with leprosy	_ _ _ _ _ OUS
Resentful of the happiness of another	_ _ _ _ OUS
Made with much care; intricate	_ _ _ _ _ OUS
Dilapidated	_ _ _ _ _ OUS
Wanton; dissolute	_ _ _ _ _ OUS
Upset over losing someone's affection	_ _ _ _ OUS
Marvelous	_ _ _ _ _ OUS
Dangerous	_ _ _ _ _ OUS
Burdensome; painful	_ _ _ _ _ OUS
Excessively eager to possess	_ _ _ _ _ OUS
Excellent; splendid	_ _ _ _ _ OUS
Morally good	_ _ _ _ _ OUS
Very valuable	_ _ _ _ _ OUS
Kind; merciful	_ _ _ _ _ OUS
Noisy	_ _ _ _ _ _ OUS
Just	_ _ _ _ _ _ OUS
Commanding	_ _ _ _ _ _ OUS
Having an abundance	_ _ _ _ _ _ OUS
Harboring ill will	_ _ _ _ _ _ OUS
Full of affliction or disorder	_ _ _ _ _ _ OUS
Pertaining to worship of false gods	_ _ _ _ _ _ _ _ OUS
Destructive	_ _ _ _ _ _ _ OUS
Disorderly; agitated	_ _ _ _ _ _ _ _ OUS
Renouncing lawful authority	_ _ _ _ _ _ _ OUS
Quarrelsome	_ _ _ _ _ _ _ _ OUS
Unnecessary	_ _ _ _ _ _ _ _ OUS
Betraying trust	_ _ _ _ _ _ _ _ OUS
Irreverent or reproachful toward God	_ _ _ _ _ _ _ _ OUS

Word List:

BLASPHEMOUS
CLAMOROUS
CONTENTIOUS
COVETOUS
CURIOUS
ENVIOUS
GLORIOUS
GRACIOUS
GRIEVOUS
IDOLATROUS
IMPERIOUS
JEALOUS
LEPROUS
MALICIOUS
PERILOUS
PERNICIOUS
PLENTEOUS
PRECIOUS
REBELLIOUS
RIGHTEOUS
RIOTOUS
RUINOUS
SUPERFLUOUS
TREACHEROUS
TROUBLOUS
TUMULTUOUS
VIRTUOUS
WONDROUS

Solution p. 120

Puzzle Solutions

Decryption

#1
Philippians 2:8

1. Prophesy
2. Vagabond
3. Manifold
4. Concubine
5. Fugitive
6. Banishment
7. Parched
8. Satiate
9. Populous

#2
2 Thessalonians 1:12

1. Jeopardy
2. Paramour
3. Ignorance
4. Stealth
5. Silverling
6. Delectable
7. Crucify
8. Ambushment
9. Sacrifice

#3
Joshua 6:2

1. Advocate
2. Pavilion
3. Holden
4. Multitude
5. Heaviness
6. Reckoning
7. Signify
8. Javelin
9. Heretick

#4
1 Samuel 1:16

1. Breeches
2. Forsaken
3. Voluntary
4. Company
5. Pilgrimage
6. Straitened
7. Purified
8. Consumption
9. Hypocrisy

Ladders

1. Gad
2. Drag
3. Ought
4. Err
5. Hire
6. Privy
7. Maw
8. Maul
9. Mount
10. Sow
11. Horn
12. Locks
13. Ark
14. Mark
15. Brink
16. Chapt
17. Heath
18. Light
19. Vaunt
20. Scum
21. Muse
22. Zeal
23. Agony
24. Plant
25. Wen
26. Espy
27. Glean

Pinwheels

#1
1. Muster
2. Schism
3. Maimed
4. Marred
5. Marrow
6. Diadem
7. Batter
8. Ravish
9. Pillar
10. Cumber
11. Doctor
12. Shiver
13. Fining
14. Coping
15. Galley
16. Girdle
17. Bowing
18. Lowing

#2
1. Botch
2. Couch
3. Hough
4. Heave
5. Helve
6. Pitch
7. Watch
8. Smith
9. Withs
10. Press
11. Stock
12. Sherd
13. Swarm
14. Viols
15. Gross
16. Dross
17. Fence
18. Grove
19. Elect
20. Nitre
21. Chide
22. Swine
23. Grave
24. Clave

#3
1. Parcel
2. Pledge
3. Pacify
4. Peeled
5. Pillar
6. Collop
7. Bonnet
8. Suburb
9. Blains
10. Belied
11. Brasen
12. Banish
13. Seethe
14. Shroud
15. Staves
16. Strait
17. Flakes
18. Clouts

Double Trouble

#1
1. glutton
2. settle
3. crossway
4. sabbath
5. array
6. commission
7. battlement
8. litters
9. suffice
10. stammering
11. myrrh
12. scabbard
13. supple
14. succeed
15. murrain
16. tillage
17. fetters
18. bellow
19. utterance
20. distaff
21. cunning
22. afflict
23. stiffen
24. bdellium
25. ambassage

#2
1. harrows
2. villany
3. stagger
4. cassia
5. mattock
6. gallows
7. accursed
8. intercessor
9. ruddy
10. pedigree
11. supplant
12. Thummim
13. occurrent
14. communicate
15. roller
16. gallant
17. traffick
18. bellows
19. harness
20. swoon
21. lattice
22. sottish
23. spittle
24. possess
25. oppression

Finish the Word Answers

#1	#2	#3	#4	#5	#6
ENDUE	DEFER	REMIT	MUNITION	WHOLLY	EXTORTION
ENSUE	DEVOUR	RENDER	VEXATION	HOLILY	COMMOTION
ENDURE	DECEASE	REVIVE	PETITION	VERILY	DAMNATION
ENCAMP	DECLINE	REBUKE	OBLATION	WILILY	EMULATION
ENTICE	DECEIVE	REPENT	SEDITION	UTTERLY	MODERATION
ENJOIN	DELIVER	REVOLT	EXACTION	PRIVILY	CONTENTION
ENVIRON	DEFRAUD	RECKON	VOCATION	CHIEFLY	ESTIMATION
ENTREAT		RESORT	DIVINATION	HASTILY	REDEMPTION
ENLARGE	DISCERN	REGARD	VISITATION	LOFTILY	DISCRETION
	DISDAIN	RETAIN	COGITATION	ROUGHLY	SUBJECTION
COMPEL	DISQUIET	RECOUNT	AFFLICTION	STRAITLY	REFORMATION
CONFER	DISANNUL	RESTORE	DESOLATION	BITTERLY	INSPIRATION
CONVEY	DISSEMBLE	REQUIRE	HABITATION	UNSEEMLY	TRANSLATION
COMMUNE	DISFIGURE	REPROACH	CORRUPTION	UNTIMELY	DECLARATION
CONDUCT		REHEARSE	LAMENTATION	MORTALLY	PROVOCATION
CONGEAL		REVERENCE	CONSOLATION	SUBTILLY	INDIGNATION
CONSUME	PROMOTE	RECONCILE	FORNICATION	HAUGHTILY	DISPUTATION
CONTEND	PROVOKE		ABOMINATION	PRESENTLY	RESTITUTION
COMMEND	PREVENT	BEHOVE	EDIFICATION	UPRIGHTLY	TRIBULATION
CORRUPT	PROLONG	BEHEAD	INQUISITION	ASSUREDLY	IMAGINATION
CONCLUDE	PROCURE	BEFALL	DISTRIBUTION	SKILFULLY	CONVOCATION
CONCEIVE	PROSPER	BESTOW	SUPPLICATION	VALIANTLY	EXHORTATION
CONFOUND	PROCLAIM	BETROTH	PROCLAMATION	EARNESTLY	PROPITIATION
CONVINCE	PROPHESY	BESEECH	CONVERSATION	DELICATELY	CONFISCATION
		BEREAVE	DISSIMULATION	STEDFASTLY	SATISFACTION
		BETHINK	SIGNIFICATION	CONTINUALLY	DISPENSATION
			SUPERSCRIPTION	COMFORTABLY	MINISTRATION
			RECONCILIATION	EXCEEDINGLY	CONFIRMATION
			INTERPRETATION	SUMPTUOUSLY	PURIFICATION
			ADMINISTRATION	UNWITTINGLY	

#7	#8
VANITY	LEPROUS
EQUITY	ENVIOUS
VERITY	CURIOUS
ENMITY	RUINOUS
NATIVITY	RIOTOUS
INIQUITY	JEALOUS
FIDELITY	WONDROUS
HUMILITY	PERILOUS
AFFINITY	GRIEVOUS
OBSCURITY	COVETOUS
SOLEMNITY	GLORIOUS
ANTIQUITY	VIRTUOUS
POSTERITY	PRECIOUS
CAPTIVITY	GRACIOUS
INFIRMITY	CLAMOROUS
MALIGNITY	RIGHTEOUS
NECESSITY	IMPERIOUS
ADVERSITY	PLENTEOUS
INTEGRITY	MALICIOUS
VIRGINITY	TROUBLOUS
PERPLEXITY	IDOLATROUS
PROSPERITY	PERNICIOUS
PARTIALITY	TUMULTUOUS
SIMPLICITY	REBELLIOUS
SUPERFLUITY	CONTENTIOUS
IMPORTUNITY	SUPERFLUOUS
HOSPITALITY	TREACHEROUS
	BLASPHEMOUS

Sort Them Out Solutions

#1

Money: Shekel, Mite, Gerah, Maneh

Plants: Hemlock, Flax, Bramble, Cockle

Trees: Almug, Algum, Juniper, Chestnut

Stones: Beryl, Sardonyx, Chrysoprasus, Carbuncle

Measurements: Hin, Ephah, Furlong, Cubit

#2

Money: Bekah, Penny, Farthing, Talent

Plants: Hyssop, Flag, Mallow, Thistle

Trees: Sycomore, Sycamine, Gopher, Hazel

Stones: Chalcedony, Agate, Ligure, Jacinth

Measurements: Firkin, Omer, Bath, Log

#3

Animals: Chamois, Pygarg, Leviathan, Behemoth

Plants: Mandrake, Nettle, Wormwood, Bulrush

Trees: Shittim, Myrtle, Teil, Willow

Stones: Chrysolyte, Sardius, Jasper, Sardine

Measurements: Homer, Cab, Span, Fathom

A to Z #1

A. Admiration
B. Boisterous
C. Circumcision
D. Predestinate
E. Engrafted
F. Affectionately
G. Diligently
H. Furtherance
I. Immutability
J. Injurious
K. Kindred
L. Illuminate
M. Contemptible
N. Incontinent
O. Conformable
P. Propitiation
Q. Banquetings
R. Regeneration
S. Stedfastness
T. Importunity
U. Disputings
V. Variableness
W. Whomsoever
X. Exceeding
Y. Presbytery
Z. Beelzebub

A to Z #2

A. Astrologer
B. Forbearance
C. Confederacy
D. Premeditate
E. Comprehend
F. Sufficiency
G. Synagogue
H. Triumphing
I. Impenitent
J. Jangling
K. Meekness
L. Infallible
M. Remembrance
N. Countenance
O. Obeisance
P. Apprehended
Q. Acquaintance
R. Foreordained
S. Superfluity
T. Translation
U. Tribulation
V. Vengeance
W. Bulwark
X. Expound
Y. Phylacteries
Z. Gazingstock

A to Z #3

A. Assurance
B. Cherubim
C. Conspiracy
D. Destitute
E. Shamefacedness
F. Sufficient
G. Outgoings
H. Replenish
I. Imagination
J. Sojourn
K. Acknowledge
L. Lasciviousness
M. Murmurings
N. Inhabitant
O. Recompence
P. Partiality
Q. Require
R. Repentance
S. Besought
T. Temperance
U. Continually
V. Advantage
W. Wormwood
X. Betwixt
Y. Tranquillity
Z. Amazement

A to Z #4

A. Aloof
B. Cumbrance
C. Concision
D. Dismayed
E. Estranged
F. Affright
G. Ingathering
H. Hoised
I. Strivings
J. Jubile
K. Breakings
L. Lurking
M. Plummet
N. Shunned
O. Occasion
P. Prognosticator
Q. Quick
R. Artificer
S. Asswage
T. Testament
U. Conduit
V. Victuals
W. Frowardness
X. Extinct
Y. Blasphemy
Z. Zealous

A to Z #5

A. Amiable
B. Abjects
C. Chronicle
D. Distracted
E. Enchantments
F. Sufficiently
G. Sluggard
H. Churlish
I. Minish
J. Justify
K. Kneadingtroughs
L. Comfortable
M. Minstrel
N. Necromancer
O. Oppressor
P. Presumptuously
Q. Quarries
R. Progenitors
S. Bloodguiltiness
T. Attendance
U. Unsavoury
V. Vehement
W. Workmanship
X. Expences
Y. Byway
Z. Hazarded

Select-A-Syllable

#1	#2	#3	#4	#5	#6
1. Abhor	1. Utter	1. Limit	1. Bosom	1. Champaign	1. Pourtray
2. Begat	2. Waver	2. Liken	2. Whoso	2. Vintage	2. Bestead
3. Adjure	3. Abate	3. Elect	3. Token	3. Firstling	3. Sustain
4. Beckon	4. Bowels	4. Tarry	4. Enjoin	4. Concourse	4. Hostage
5. Buffet	5. Devout	5. Afresh	5. Surety	5. Journey	5. Laden
6. Decree	6. Favour	6. Censer	6. Tribute	6. Transgress	6. Fashion
7. Coffer	7. Figure	7. Deceit	7. Succour	7. Heathen	7. Stately
8. Impart	8. Ascend	8. Lively	8. Offence	8. Sackbut	8. Quarter
9. Record	9. Bramble	9. Suffer	9. Mingled	9. Casement	9. Garnish
10. Manger	10. Chamber	10. Brawler	10. Subject	10. Inward	10. Subscribe
11. Savour	11. Consent	11. Clamour	11. Torment	11. Graving	11. Treason
12. Tumult	12. Fulfill	12. Compass	12. Charger	12. Receipt	12. Dungeon
13. Redeem	13. Latchet	13. Froward	13. Oppress	13. Acquaint	13. Parlour
14. Virtue	14. Rubbish	14. Madness	14. Unction	14. Threshold	14. Incline
15. Blemish	15. Possess	15. Noisome	15. Beguile	15. Remnant	15. Augment
16. Bullock	16. Prating	16. Blasting	16. Contrite	16. Tidings	16. Cracknel
17. Certain	17. Publish	17. Conceive	17. Flourish	17. Frontlet	17. Timbrel
18. Captive	18. Rampart	18. Dreadful	18. Hireling	18. Jealous	18. Stripling
19. Doleful	19. Servile	19. Fragment	19. Languish	19. Harness	19. Conclude
20. Gentile	20. Smitten	20. Mischief	20. Venture	20. Bolster	20. Carcase

Down the Stairs Solutions

#1	#2	#3	#4	#5
1. Savour	1. Rebuke	1. Latter	1. Novice	1. Equity
2. Estate	2. Ground	2. Albeit	2. Anoint	2. Descry
3. Visage	3. Verity	3. Hallow	3. Gender	3. Amends
4. Vessel	4. Dearth	4. Fowler	4. Stanch	4. Bowels
5. Dropsy	5. Allure	5. Simple	5. Talent	5. Badger
6. Ouches	6. Wither	6. Shekel	6. Wanton	6. Indite
7. Sought	7. Reject	7. Lintel	7. Nether	7. Encamp
8. Astray	8. Oracle	8. Cleave	8. Endued	8. Felloe
9. Desert	9. Thresh	9. Holpen	9. Vanity	9. Fleece
10. Damsel	10. Emerod	10. Fallow	10. Thongs	10. Desert
11. Famish	11. Sundry	11. Kindle	11. Famine	11. Socket
12. Whelps	12. Temper	12. Carnal	12. Sodden	12. Scribe
13. Seemly	13. Renown	13. Leaven	13. Nought	13. Ensign
14. Esteem	14. Breach	14. Plague	14. Enmity	14. Devise
15. Custom	15. Thrice	15. Colour	15. Sunder	15. Amerce
16. Noised	16. Charge	16. Harlot	16. Garner	16. Surety
17. Vanish	17. Covert	17. Mingle	17. Abound	17. Porter
18. Taches	18. Canker	18. Subtil	18. Molten	18. Charge
19. Stocks	19. Revive	19. Lament	19. Nobles	19. Earing
20. Psalms	20. Oracle	20. Cloven	20. Endure	20. Heifer
21. Custom	21. Murmur	21. Solemn	21. Yonder	21. Beeves
22. Chaste	22. Matrix	22. Fillet	22. Signet	22. Remedy
23. Oppose	23. Endure	23. Goodly	23. Offend	23. Pommel
24. Hedges	24. Valour	24. Mutual	24. Bidden	24. Humble

Missing Vowels

#1	#2
whence	herein
wherefore	whilst
likewise	hereunto
therefrom	wheresoever
therewith	notwithstanding
fain	wherewithal
howbeit	insomuch
wherein	whereunto
thereby	aright
whereon	hither
moreover	therein
whither	albeit
henceforward	whithersoever
nigh	nevertheless
whereinsoever	forsomuch
hereafter	thereunto
oftentimes	oft
withal	afore
inasmuch	straightway
whereas	insomuch
henceforth	anon
hitherto	thereon
thereof	forasmuch
peradventure	soever
aforetime	thence
wherewith	unawares
whereof	heretofore
thereout	forthwith
thither	betimes

Word Search

P	H	L	Y	L	E	U	W	N	L	L	K	Y	J	M
Q	L	U	Z	U	O	Q	O	H	W	N	T	Y	M	R
Z	E	A	Z	K	Y	R	W	U	N	F	J	U	L	U
A	D	H	J	S	M	G	Y	P	S	T	L	E	E	Y
P	S	J	M	R	B	Y	A	R	T	E	B	N	N	D
K	P	T	T	Y	V	K	R	P	R	D	G	W	O	C
J	D	R	O	W	V	B	T	R	E	R	E	I	M	O
U	F	E	U	N	C	C	X	I	A	G	R	D	S	P
Y	E	A	L	J	I	J	H	V	K	C	L	O	H	E
J	D	T	G	T	D	S	E	A	D	K	T	A	L	E
L	O	B	O	D	O	E	H	T	M	Q	Q	O	R	L
Y	R	P	E	L	E	I	P	E	U	P	A	B	B	Y
L	M	I	I	Y	A	R	N	L	D	D	A	L	B	O
K	M	A	R	S	H	Z	A	Y	E	Y	I	I	V	E
K	L	X	Q	X	S	L	S	D	B	H	M	B	N	O

ASTONISHED
BID
BETRAY
CHAMPAIN
DARED
TREAT
ENGRAVE
HAUL
HELPED
LOADED
MARSH
PEEL
PRIVATELY
RYE
STREAK
SIP

Snowflakes Solutions

#1
1. Laver
2. Ravin
3. Sever
7. Besom
8. Issue
9. Haste
13. Slain
14. Chaff
15. Exalt
19. Twain
20. Abase
21. Frame

Bible Word: Remnant

#2
1. Mitre
2. Utter
3. Altar
7. Alter
8. Extol
9. Tithe
13. Feign
14. Guile
15. Amiss
19. Haply
20. Viper
21. Piped

Bible Word: Prudently

#3
1. Frame
2. Avail
3. Gnash
7. Image
8. Realm
9. Scall
13. Grope
14. Score
15. Shock
19. Assay
20. Lusty
21. Visit

Bible Word: Villages

#4
1. Churl
2. Usury
3. Couch
7. Ephah
8. Ephod
9. Abhor
13. Clods
14. Odour
15. Stock
19. Booth
20. Wroth
21. Stout

Bible Word: Breaches

#5
1. Amend
2. Cleft
3. Sheet
7. Yield
8. Stead
9. Wrest
13. Edify
14. Loins
15. Reins
19. Beryl
20. Wares
21. Peril

Bible Word: Psaltery

#6
1. Court
2. Haunt
3. Bruit
7. Palsy
8. Folly
9. Pulse
13. Brute
14. Sound
15. Usurp
19. Cloke
20. Sport
21. Thorn

Bible Word: Speeches

#7
1. Grave
2. Slack
3. Snare
7. Goads
8. Exact
9. Chafe
13. Range
14. Tenon
15. Wench
19. Mirth
20. Tares
21. Durst

Bible Word: Eschewed

One of Each
1. herald
2. woeful
3. justle
4. curdle
5. strive
6. covert
7. retire
8. flagon
9. cornet
10. depose
11. course
12. graven
13. scurvy

Compound Words

#1
1. W
2. U
3. CC
4. M
5. BB
6. P
7. B
8. K
9. I
10. Q
11. R
12. N
13. J
14. Y
15. AA
16. V
17. Z
18. E
19. C
20. T
21. S
22. G
23. O
24. H
25. D
26. L
27. DD
28. F
29. A
30. X

#2
1. Z
2. T
3. M
4. R
5. X
6. O
7. N
8. J
9. Y
10. I
11. AA
12. Q
13. V
14. BB
15. B
16. CC
17. F
18. A
19. G
20. K
21. W
22. DD
23. U
24. L
25. S
26. H
27. C
28. D
29. P
30. E

#3
1. DD
2. T
3. A
4. Z
5. R
6. D
7. M
8. S
9. V
10. H OR I
11. AA
12. N
13. L
14. H OR I
15. E
16. X
17. BB
18. CC
19. G
20. F
21. W
22. C
23. O
24. K
25. Y
26. U
27. B
28. J
29. Q
30. P

Secret Word Solutions

#1
Fast	Prey
Hoar	Meek
Muse	Hale
Base	Paps
FAME	REAP
Gird	Dumb
Bray	Tale
Lees	Rase
Wise	Stay
DREW	BEST
Fowl	Hind
Heed	Quit
Halt	Rent
Gall	Trow
WELL	DIRT

#2
Rail	Horn
Stay	Rear
Yoke	Riot
Tell	Rend
LAKE	RAIN
List	Vale
Poll	Wean
Sown	Shew
Dote	Trod
LOST	LAST
Deck	Alms
Shod	Meet
Vile	Reed
Miry	Nigh
DOER	AMEN

#3
Fray	Mite
Knop	Lade
Mote	Quit
Stay	Dash
ROOT	MAID
Oath	Wist
Want	Flay
Gain	Vail
Mire	Halt
HAIR	WAIT
Mete	Wont
Fain	Meat
Flax	Whit
Poll	Tell
TILL	NAIL

#4
Vial	Pitch
Trow	Midst
Cast	Lothe
Save	Piety
LOSE	PITY
Wail	Smite
Pomp	Sound
Sect	Thine
Cock	Press
LOCK	MOTE
Lust	Bough
Slay	Jewry
Meat	Sware
Spue	Adder
LAMP	BEAR

#5
Rush	Rank
Ague	Reel
Urim	Tale
Save	Ward
SAME	NEAR
Puff	Dale
Aloe	Lice
Mess	Fens
Vain	Deal
PLEA	LIED
Dram	Pill
Warp	Boil
Sore	Haft
Lean	Lien
RASE	LIFE

#6
Ward	Levy
Daub	Ciel
Balm	Envy
Tell	Wood
WALL	VIEW
Woof	Cote
Crop	Wave
Caul	Bade
Mail	Onyx
FOAM	OVEN
Rank	Bank
Void	Pare
Mown	Gape
Hewn	Pate
KINE	KEPT

Cookie Sheets

#1
Steward Instant Travail Situate
Chastise Astonied Partaker Impudent
Attentive Immutable Remission Weariness
Wrought Sanctify Subvert Disciple

#2
Anguish Notable Furbish Gravity
Variance Rudiment Beautify Subtilty
Barbarous Continual Infirmity Perplexed
Forbear Pleasant Gainsay Vigilant

#3
Arrayed Strawed Conceit Diverse
Desirous Grievous Plaister Untoward
Diligence Revelling Substance Accompany
Austere Assented Fervent Accursed

#4
Forgive Infidel Billows Banquet
Covenant Desolate Dwelling Exploits
Adversary Adversity Unfeigned Trembling
Draught Flattery Magnify Lunatick

#5
Scourge Portion Grisled Inquire
Endeavor Profound Riddance Sobriety
Estranged Vengeance Spikenard Slaughter
Sensual Clemency Riotous Infinite

Picture Match

#1	#2
1. C	1. P
2. E	2. J
3. P	3. N
4. I	4. D
5. A	5. F
6. J	6. E
7. K	7. A
8. B	8. B
9. H	9. L
10. F	10. C
11. N	11. G
12. D	12. H
13. M	13. O
14. G	14. M
15. O	15. I
16. L	16. K
17. G	

Old Verb Endings

1. Anointed
2. Bless
3. Blesses
4. Borrows
5. Cares
6. Commit
7. Creeps
8. Cry
9. Divides
10. Exalt
11. Fill
12. Forgave
13. Glories
14. Laid
15. Moved
16. Multiply
17. Open
18. Prepare
19. Read
20. Runs
21. Smooths
22. Supplies
23. Upbraids
24. Wins

Anagrams

#1
1. chapter
2. treacherous
3. Pentecost
4. stature
5. substance
6. teraphim
7. provender
8. innumerable
9. constraint
10. concupiscence
11. forbearing
12. chariot
13. necessity
14. publican
15. abundant
16. desolate
17. exhortation
18. mariners
19. stubble
20. suborned
21. testator
22. patriarch
23. apothecary

#2
1. sacrilege
2. superfluous
3. brutish
4. appearance
5. consecrate
6. tabernacle
7. abolish
8. sabaoth
9. wreathen
10. impute
11. calamities
12. enlightened
13. confirmation
14. dispensation
15. surmisings
16. surname
17. fatling
18. profane
19. sanctuary
20. evangelist
21. slanderer
22. solitary

#3
1. venison
2. proselyte
3. transfigure
4. continuance
5. perilous
6. adamant
7. blaspheme
8. inordinate
9. purloining
10. malefactors
11. inspiration
12. swaddling
13. incorruptible
14. comeliness
15. pertain
16. gluttonous
17. impoverished
18. certain
19. draught
20. potentate
21. carbuncle
22. chargeable
23. dissension

#4
1. affrighted
2. precious
3. parable
4. pestilence
5. vehement
6. residue
7. plenteous
8. prosperous
9. persecute
10. traitor
11. pottage
12. leasing
13. hypocrite
14. alienated
15. heritage
16. witness
17. contentious
18. surfeiting
19. intercession
20. implacable
21. disallowed
22. magistrate

#5
1. asunder
2. baptism
3. burning
4. dandled
5. garrison
6. imagery
7. leprosy
8. mollified
9. scourge
10. valiant
11. wrought
12. detestable
13. sleight
14. respite
15. mortify
16. mastery
17. learned
18. hungred
19. forfeit
20. drought
21. coulter
22. bondage
23. ascribe

#6
1. avouched
2. begotten
3. espousals
4. familiar
5. impotent
6. leavened
7. manifest
8. meditate
9. ravening
10. seraphims
11. advertise
12. artillery
13. broidered
14. estranged
15. incurable
16. obstinate
17. jeoparded
18. constrain
19. sodering
20. slothful
21. prudence
22. peculiar
23. minister

#7
1. displeasure
2. deliverance
3. untempered
4. unsatiable
5. suretiship
6. straitness
7. putrifying
8. outlandish
9. magnifical
10. intreaties
11. execration
12. distribute
13. cockatrice
14. brigandine
15. adulteress
16. vermilion
17. tributary
18. remainder
19. patrimony
20. habitable
21. genealogy
22. feignedly

Synonym Scramble Answers

#1

BESIEGE	BESET
COMPASS	INCLOSE
CHASTEN	CHASTISE
CORRECT	AFFLICT
RANSOM	REDEEM
DELIVER	RESCUE
SUBDUE	DISCOMFIT
PREVAIL	CONQUER
GARMENT	RAIMENT
VESTURE	VESTMENT
HEED	ATTEND
REGARD	HEARKEN

#2

INIQUITY	TRANSGRESSION
OFFENCE	TRESPASS
CONTEMN	DESPISE
ABHOR	REJECT
APPOINT	ESTABLISH
ORDAIN	STABLISH
LET	SUFFER
ALLOW	PERMIT
BEMOAN	MOURN
REPENT	REGRET
PRUDENT	DISCREET
CIRCUMSPECT	WARE

#3

TEMPT	PROVE
TRY	EXAMINE
BEWRAY	SHEW
BETRAY	DISCLOSE
CHOLER	FURY
INDIGNATION	WRATH
COMMANDMENT	PRECEPT
STATUTE	ORDINANCE
IGNOMINY	INFAMY
REPROACH	DISGRACE
PERFECTLY	WHOLLY
CLEAN	UTTERLY

#4

LUCRE	GAIN
PROSPERITY	MAMMON
SIMILITUDE	RESEMBLANCE
LIKENESS	IMAGE
COMELY	CONVENIENT
MEET	SEEMLY
ANON	FORTHWITH
STRAIGHTWAY	IMMEDIATELY
REQUITE	RECOMPENSE
AVENGE	RETALIATE
SUPPLICATION	INTREATY
PETITION	PRAYER

Crossword 1

Crossword 2

Crossword 3

Crossword 4

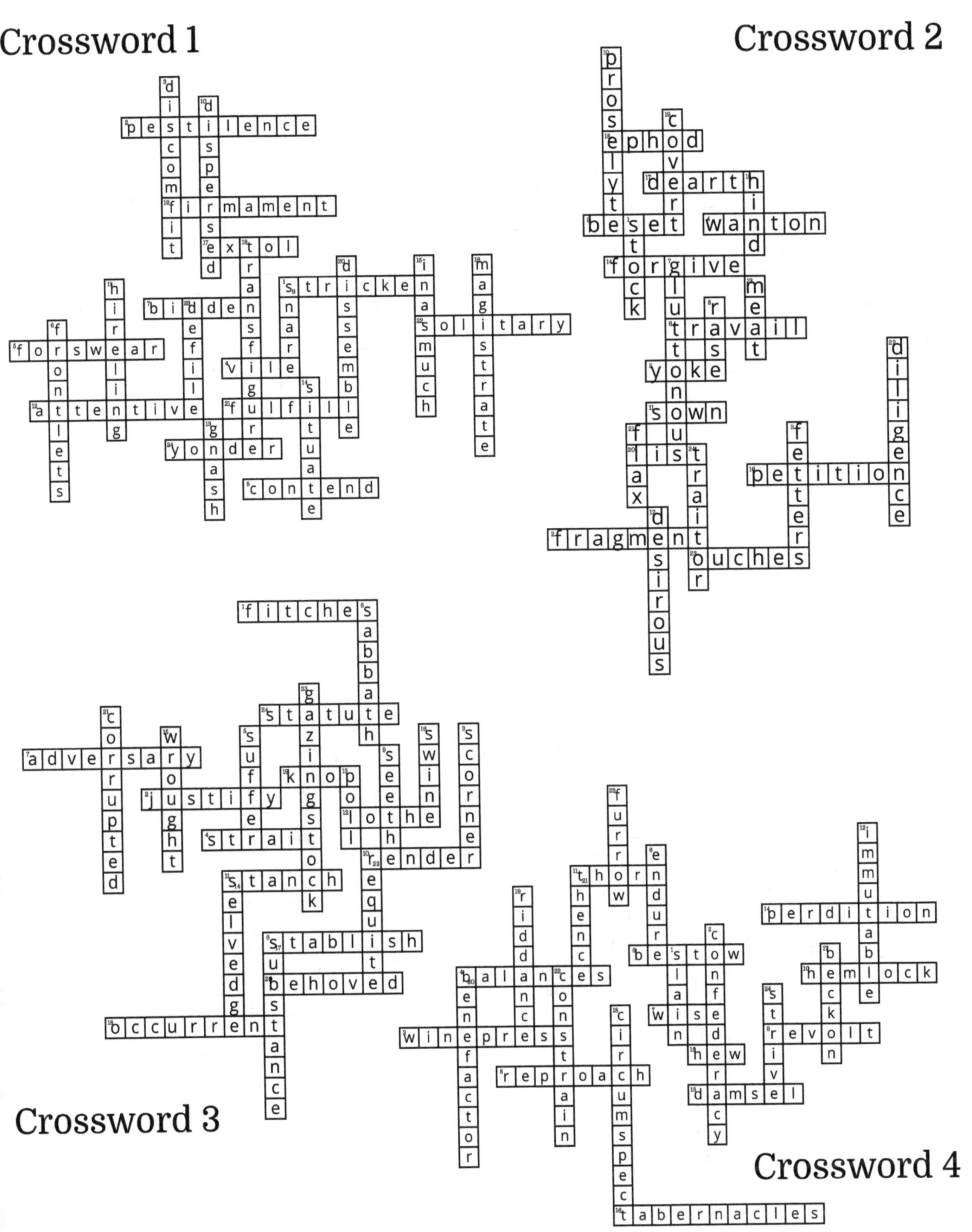

Crossword 5

Crossword 6

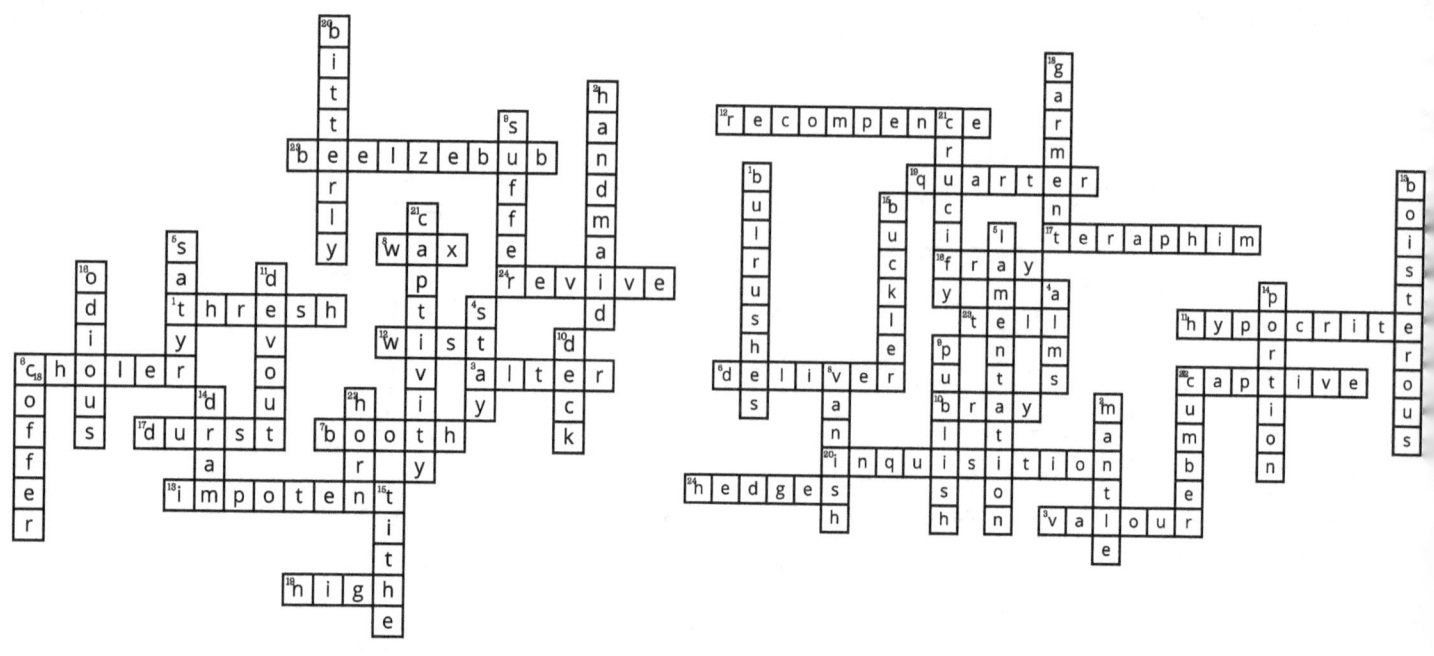

Crossword 7

Crossword 8

Crossword 9

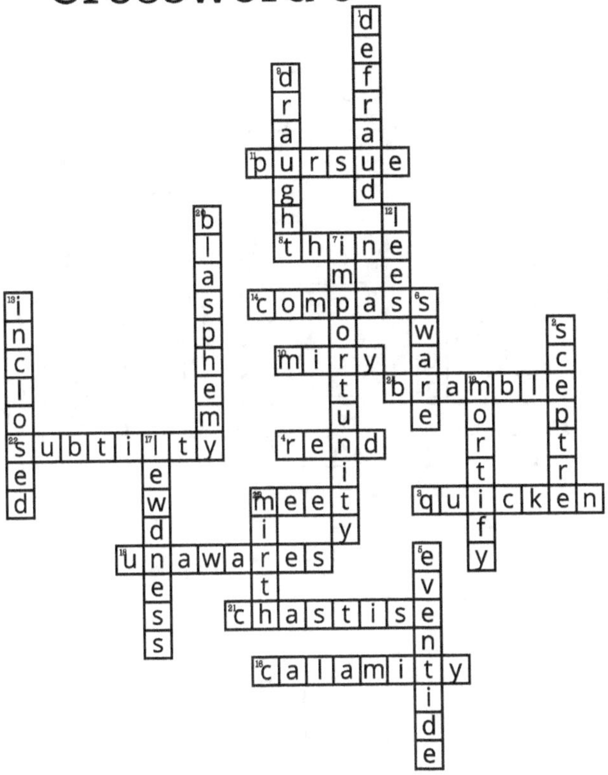

Crossword 10

Crossword 11

Crossword 12

Crossword 13

Crossword 14

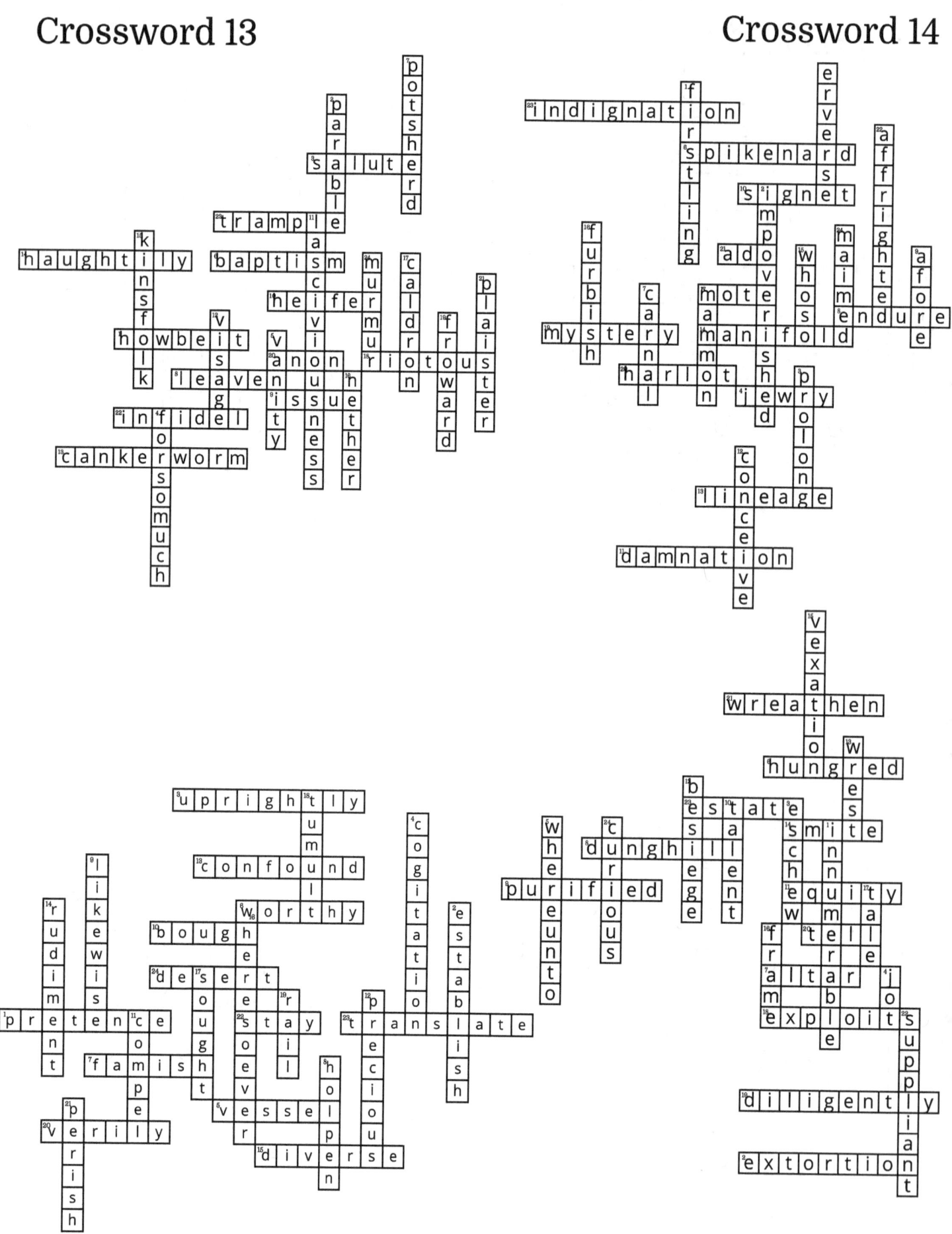

Crossword 15

Crossword 16

Crossword 17

Crossword 18

Crossword 19

Crossword 20

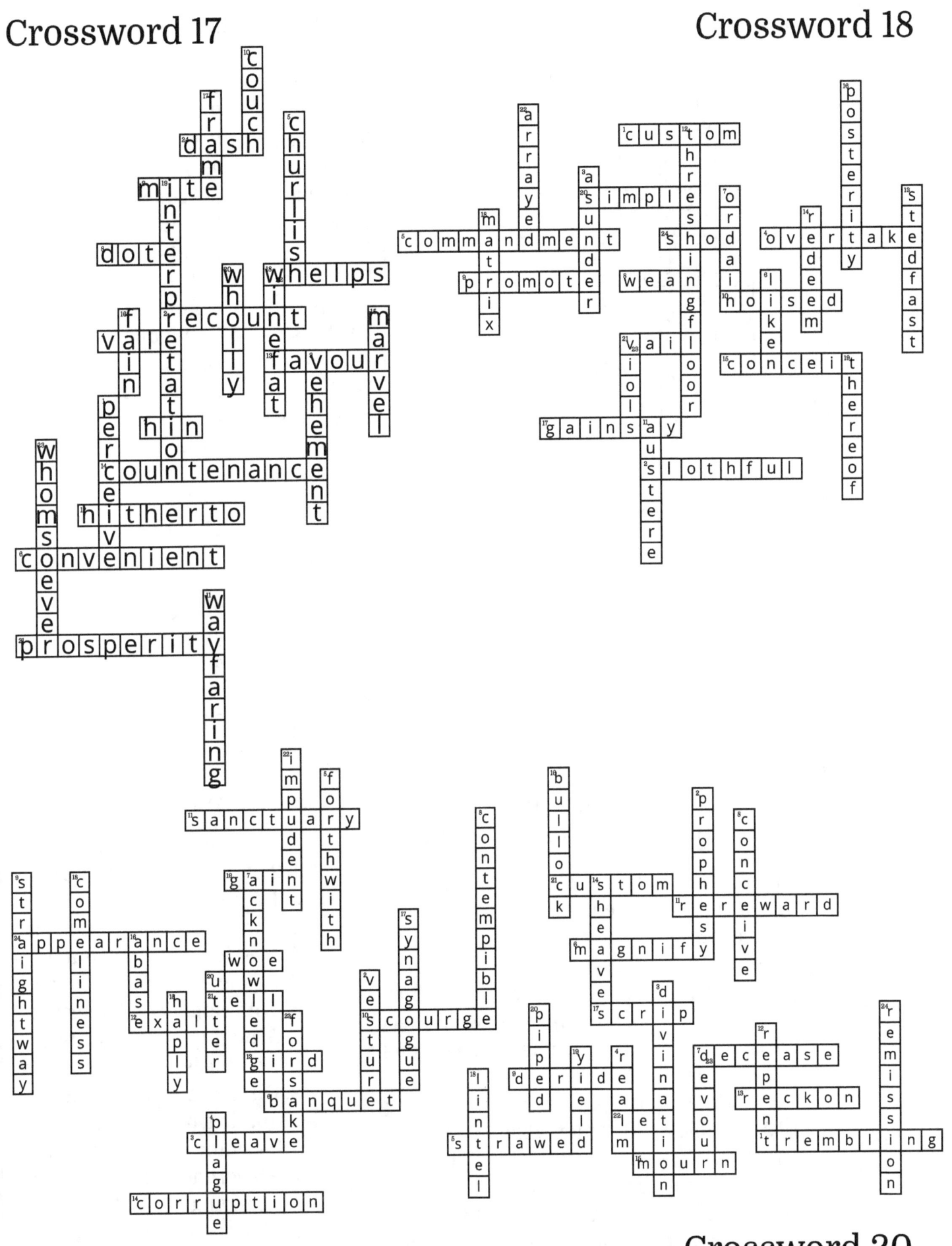

Crossword 21

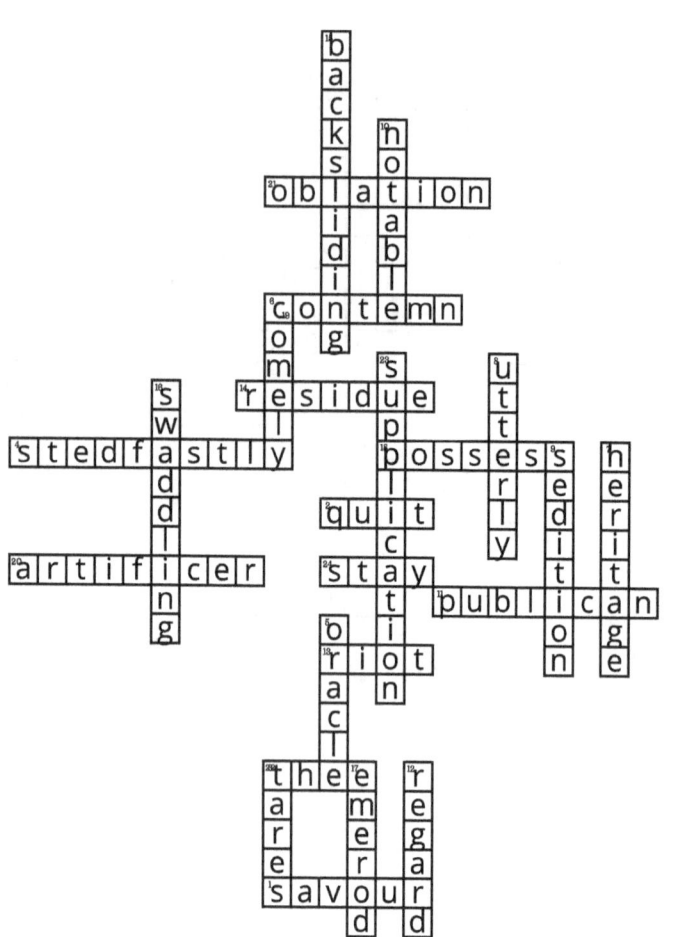

Caterpillars

#1	#2
1. Virtue	1. Vessel
2. Ere	2. Lad
3. Eunuch	3. Distil
4. Hew	4. Let
5. Wallow	5. Trusty
6. Wax	6. You
7. Ado	7. Aul
8. Odious	8. League
9. Sop	9. Ear
10. Perish	10. Rigour
11. Hap	11. Ram
12. Pursue	12. Meddle
13. Furrow	13. Embalm
14. Woe	14. Mar
15. Eschew	15. Rising
16. Wot	16. Gat
17. Throng	17. Target
18. Gin	18. Thy
19. Jot	19. Apt
20. Twined	20. Tablet
21. Dam	21. Tow
22. Marvel	22. Winnow
23. Let	23. Wit
24. Tittle	24. Thrust

Plural or Singular?

1. P
2. P
3. P
4. P
5. S
6. S
7. P
8. S
9. S
10. P
11. S
12. P
13. S

Common Denominator

#1	#2	#3
1. morsel	1. quench	1. certify
2. worthy	2. lentiles	2. cistern
3. discord	3. ravenous	3. diviner
4. exactor	4. reverend	4. proverb
5. forsake	5. purtenance	5. scorner
6. fortify	6. recompense	6. adultery
7. scorner	7. enlargement	7. kerchief
8. worthies	8. avenger	8. perverse
9. tenor	9. unleavened	9. tabering
10. forcible	10. lamentable	10. bravery
11. inferior	11. lieutenant	11. calkers
12. mediator	12. degenerate	12. countervail
13. mortgage	13. enflaming	13. conversant
14. foreigner	14. pretence	14. chamberlain
15. ignorance	15. revenue	15. confederate

Daisy Chain

#1	#2
1. Standard	1. Snuffers
2. Dainties	2. Sodomite
3. Scrabble	3. Endamage
4. Election	4. Eloquent
5. Negligent	5. Tirshatha
6. Tottering	6. Appertain
7. Grudging	7. Neesings
8. Godliness	8. Soundness
9. Displease	9. Effectual
10. Endeavors	10. Loathsome
11. Servitor	11. Espoused
12. Reverence	12. Dayspring
13. Enticing	13. Gracious
14. Governor	14. Scaffold
15. Recorder	15. Drunkard
16. Rereward	16. Desolate